Texas Political Memorabilia

NUMBER ELEVEN
Clifton and Shirley Caldwell Texas Heritage Series

Texas Political Memorabilia

BUTTONS, BUMPER STICKERS, AND BROADSIDES

Chuck Bailey with *Bill Crawford*

FOREWORD BY PAUL BURKA   PHOTOGRAPHS BY BARBARA SCHLIEF

UNIVERSITY OF TEXAS PRESS, AUSTIN

Publication of this work was made possible in part by support from Clifton and Shirley Caldwell and a challenge grant from the National Endowment for the Humanities.

LIBRARY OF CONGRESS CATALOGING-IN-PUBLICATION DATA

Bailey, Chuck
Texas political memorabilia / by Chuck Bailey ; with Bill Crawford ; foreword by Paul Burka ; photographs by Barbara Schlief. — 1st ed.
p.   cm. — (Clifton and Shirley Caldwell Texas heritage series ; no. 11)
Includes bibliographical references and index.
ISBN-13: 978-0-292-71625-4 ((cl.) : alk. paper)
ISBN-10: 0-292-71625-7
1. Campaign paraphernalia—Texas. I. Crawford, Bill, 1955– II. Schlief, Barbara. III. Title.
NK3669.B35 2007
324.9764'0075—dc22   2006031432

Contents

PAUL BURKA

Foreword

Chuck Bailey's fascination with Texas campaign memorabilia started out as a hobby, but within these pages it becomes much more. Through buttons and bumper stickers and the like, Bailey has found a new way to tell the history of Texas politics. You will find material from Sam Houston to Sam Rayburn, from Joseph Bailey (Texas's first real scoundrel) to Kay Bailey Hutchison. Aficionados of Texas politics will find memories on every page.

To peruse Bailey's collection is to realize how much the business of politics has changed. Many of the items featured here date from an era when there was no television and no polls. Candidates used them as they use the mass media today: to get their names before the public. In addition to the ubiquitous buttons and bumper stickers, Bailey's collection includes lighters, matchbooks, cookbooks, fans, postcards, business cards, playing cards, neckties, dominos, pins, pens, pencils, ribbons, posters, pamphlets, rulers, golf tees, thimbles, pickles, flour sacks, shoelaces, nail files, key rings, scarves, hair clips, watches, luggage tags, name tags, dustpans, pocket knives, and newspapers. They bring Texas political history alive. One of my favorite items in Bailey's collection is the *Ferguson Forum* (page 169), a newspaper started in 1917 by the recently impeached governor, James "Pa" Ferguson (our second real scoundrel), to get his side of the story to his supporters. Later, after his wife, Miriam, won the governorship and returned him to power and influence, it was said that construction companies interested in highway contracts were well advised to buy advertising in the *Forum*.

Just as today's TV commercials create images for candidates, so did yesterday's campaign handouts. Has there ever been a better political slogan than the economical "I Like Ike" (page 55)? It contrasted the down-to-earth Republican presidential nominee of 1952, Dwight Eisenhower, with his Democratic rival

Adlai Stevenson, whose eloquence and intelligence became a liability. When Lyndon Johnson first ran for the U.S. Senate, in a 1941 special election, he handed out business cards that featured a photograph of himself alongside President Franklin Roosevelt, who a year earlier had won reelection to a third term. "Support Johnson and Roosevelt," it read. "Won't you help? Your country, yourself, and your good friend. Elect Lyndon B. Johnson U.S. Senator." Perhaps unwisely, Johnson was positioning himself as a New Deal liberal, a stance that was becoming increasingly controversial in Texas—which may explain why he lost, narrowly, to W. Lee "Pappy" O'Daniel.

Even in the TV age, politicians have continued to use campaign buttons to reinforce the way they want to be perceived by the voters. Senator Phil Gramm touted his conservative ideology in his 1996 race for reelection with two buttons (page 26), one that bore a picture of a covered wagon; another that read, simply, "Official Gramm Wagon Puller." These were references to Gramm's oft-stated line that "You're either pulling the wagon or riding in the wagon."

Items that could be worn or otherwise displayed had much the same role that polls do today. Voters could look at buttons, yard signs, and bumper stickers and get a fair idea of how a campaign was going in their neighborhood and their town. In an era when people knew their neighbors, a button on a friend's lapel could sway a vote.

It is impossible to look at Bailey's collection without feeling a tug of nostalgia for a time when politics was personal rather than ideological and voters felt strongly enough about the candidates of their choice to put their loyalties on display. I felt that I was renewing acquaintances with old friends as I leafed through the pages—none older, or a better friend, than Babe Schwartz (page 189), the state senator from my hometown of Galveston, who hired me out of law school as a legislative aide in 1968. I'm sure that I have one of those "Re-Elect A. R. 'Babe' Schwartz" rulers in some box in my garage. And, although I never met him, I still feel an affinity for "The Old Scotchman," Gordon McLendon (page 19). He made me a lifelong baseball fan with his thrilling re-creations of major league games (illegal, as it turned out) in the early fifties on the Liberty Broadcasting System.

McLendon also was a pioneer of Top Forty radio. But he is in Bailey's book because he tried, futilely, to unseat U.S. Senator Ralph W. Yarborough in the 1964 Democratic primary. I remember, too, the button, "Maybe They Meant 2 Days Every 140 Years" (page 106), which everyone in the Capitol was wearing as a particularly awful legislative session in the late eighties sputtered toward its constitutionally ordained demise.

One is reminded, too, of how soon most politicians are forgotten. Which of these names can you identify: Charley Lockhart? George Mahon? Bill Blakley? Lockhart (page 205) was a midget who served as state treasurer for ten years, from 1931 to 1941. Mahon (page 39) represented Lubbock in the U.S. Congress for forty-four years, the last fourteen of which (1964–1978) he was chairman of the House Committee on Appropriations and a symbol of Texas's power in Washington. Blakley (page 19) was appointed to the U.S. Senate by Democratic governor Price Daniel in 1961 to fill the seat vacated by LBJ, who had assumed the office of vice-president. He ran in the special election to serve the full term, but he was so conservative that liberal Democrats "went fishing" on election day. This opened the door for John Tower to become the first Republican to win a statewide election since Reconstruction. Tower would go on to serve four terms and play an essential role in the building of his party.

I have mentioned some of my favorite items in this book, but I'm pretty sure I know what Bailey's favorites are as well. Along with some nineteenth-century treasures, they would be the collection from the campaigns of the late Bob Bullock (pages 162 and 165), for whom Bailey served as chief of staff during Bullock's second term as lieutenant governor. Bullock was famously irascible and mercurial, but no one could be around him for very long without being touched by his commitment to public service and his love for Texas and Texas politics. That love, transmitted to Bailey, is reflected on every page of this book.

Introduction

On an early fall evening in 1960, my father brought me a sack of Kennedy-Johnson buttons. I took them with a smile and was glad to get them for two reasons. First, I collected coins, baseball cards, rocks, comic books, and felt pennants so I needed something else to collect. Second, and much more important, I was only one of two Kennedy-Johnson supporters in my sixth-grade class, and I was tired of seeing the numerous little red buttons with "Nixon" printed inside an outline of Texas.

I did not let partisanship, however, keep me from collecting Republican buttons, and soon I had as many Nixon-Lodge buttons as Kennedy-Johnson. This was the beginning of my political memorabilia collection, and as time passed the baseball cards, rocks, comic books, coins, and pennants fell to the wayside, while the political collection grew.

As I grew older, I became more and more interested in politics, and that interest included collecting all sorts of memorabilia from all sorts of elections. From presidential buttons, I expanded into city, county, and state buttons, bumper stickers, and posters. I also collected political bullet pencils, thimbles, peanuts, cigarettes, chewing gum, and key rings. Eventually, as any collector will tell you, it became necessary to specialize. In political memorabilia, collectors can specialize in presidential or local items. They can narrow the focus to particular candidates; concentrate on specific types of issues; or collect items from particular states and their congressional, legislative, or city and county campaigns.

While I still collect memorabilia from all presidential races, I have narrowed the rest of my collecting to Texas politics. As you'll see in this book, the often colorful, sometimes controversial, and always entertaining leaders of our state have provided a wide array of campaign artifacts. Some are truly Texan, such as the

Lyndon Johnson ashtray in the shape of a Stetson and the Ann Richards plastic cowboy boot with her name on it. Ralph Yarborough used yellow rose pins embossed with his initials, and Dolph Briscoe's campaign produced cattle ear-tags exhorting "Briscoe for Governor." W. Lee "Pappy" O'Daniel, a flour magnate, used miniature flour barrels. John Connally printed stickers saying "Elect Connally Governor" in the school colors from the old Southwest conference. Wisely, he omitted the University of Arkansas. As late as 2004, Rick Perry had lapel pins imprinted with his initials to look like a cattle brand.

Where did American political materials, this popular art of democracy, originate? From the earliest days of the nation, political trinkets such as clothing buttons, snuff boxes, straight razors, pottery, and ribbons were used during each campaign cycle. Inaugural clothing buttons were produced for George Washington. Campaign medals, often the size of a quarter, could be drilled or "holed," attached to a string, and worn on a man's lapel. With the expansion of photography in the mid-nineteenth century, ferrotype (an early type of photography) buttons were used. These were followed by cheaper, round, pin-backed buttons or shirt studs that had small photographs of candidates glued onto them. In the 1860 presidential race, this type of "button" was produced for Lincoln, Douglas, Bell, and Breckinridge, the major candidates of that pivotal election.

As the century progressed, political ribbons with pictures attached, large banners, song sheets, campaign lanterns, campaign hats, and uniforms appeared—and sometimes quickly fell into disuse. However, the ubiquitous lapel device was always around, and in 1896 the modern campaign button burst upon the scene with a vast array of styles, colors, shapes, and designs. This new button was a cel-luloid-covered picture or slogan with a pin attached to the back. Celluloid, an early plastic-like substance, allowed button manufacturers to mass produce a cheap, colorful, and durable piece of advertising. National companies such as Whitehead and Hogue, Bastien Brothers, and St. Louis Button Company sold buttons all over the country. Local Texas enterprises such as the Fred Lake Company and Weaver Badge Co., both from Dallas, filled the local need for such advertising. Before radio and television, campaigns often used posters, broadsides, and friendly newspapers to get out the message. Prior to the passage of the 19th Amendment, "Vote for Women" celluloid buttons were quite popular. With the advent of the celluloid button, "sound bites" could be worn on every man or woman's coat lapel.

Spring-loaded mechanical buttons appeared about the same time as celluloid, and in the 1920s tin lithograph lapel buttons began to appear. In the 1950s and 60s, the Vari-Vue company made buttons that showed different pictures depending on the angle from which the button was viewed. Plastic buttons and battery-operated buttons equipped with flashing lights and digitized campaign slogans and songs brought buttons into the high-tech age of the twenty-first century.

In Texas, buttons and other memorabilia have not always been abundant. Most Texas buttons from races prior to 1940 are rare—often so scarce that only one or two examples are known. Pre-twentieth-century items are almost nonexistent. A number of factors can explain this scarcity. First, Texas was a big, rural state. Its population was scattered among small towns, ranches, and farms, and it was simply hard for campaigners to get to the population. Second, after reconstruction Texas was a one-party state. To paraphrase former Lt. Governor Ben Ramsey, you would need hunting dogs to find a Republican in East Texas. And those dogs would certainly be yellow. Once the Democratic primaries were over, there was little use for political memorabilia of any kind. Finally, hard-working rural families might have had time to read a week-old newspaper or attend a Saturday afternoon stump-speech at the courthouse. What remaining leisure time they had was spent at church or the local lodge, and there is almost as much church and lodge memorabilia from that early time as there is political.

With the advent of radio and television, broadcast political ads became the new "buttons." All the advertising revenue went and still goes to the media that reach the largest population. So while buttons and bumper stickers are still available at campaign offices, they are usually for sale. Often a button jobber will make the buttons, sell them at events or headquarters, and sometimes split the money with the campaign.

In a way, buttons have come full circle since the 1896 glory days. Like the vendors at the turn of the twentieth century who walked downtown streets with placards full of celluloid masterpieces, vendors now use the internet to sell a plethora of colorful, amusing, and well-designed buttons. Instead of searching out campaign offices, supporters can turn to candidate websites or auctions and order buttons through the worldwide web. Collectors no longer have to paw through junk bins at antique stores and flea markets digging for lost treasure. Like the day my father brought home my sack of treasures, a find on the internet auction sites can bring a smile to the most experienced collector.

Are Texas items different from other states? In general, no. However, Texas candidates are more likely to have an outline of the state, a Texas State Flag or "Texans Want _____ for Governor." It is a subtle difference from other states, but one that carries forth the Texas mystique.

The politicians listed in the book are often more colorful than their memorabilia. They run the gamut from presidents to state senators, from founding fathers to the new boys on the block. Names like Austin, Houston, LBJ, Connally, Maverick, Jordan, Gonzales, Bush, and Bullock are not likely to be soon forgotten. The authors hope the memorabilia in this book guarantees that names like Wilson, O'Daniel, Jester, Garner, Wright, and all the others will stay in the memories of Texans for years to come.

Something should be said in explanation of how we picked the Texans mentioned in this book. Being an elected official was not enough. In fact, some of our candidates never ran for office in Texas. Davey Crockett, though a Tennessee congressman, is simply a larger-than-life character.

Governors, senators, house Speakers, lieutenant governors, and other politicians made the list because of leadership, quotability, personality, or political importance, and some have that intangible quality that says they could be from no place else but the Lone Star State.

The Memorabilia

PLATE 1

Lyndon Johnson

Lyndon Johnson was elected to Congress in 1937. He ran for the Senate in a 1941 special election but was defeated by Governor W. Lee "Pappy" O'Daniel. Vowing never to be politically maneuvered again, he narrowly defeated Governor Coke Stevenson for a senate seat in 1948. He became president after John Kennedy's assassination in 1963 and was elected to the office in 1964. He retired to Texas in 1969. His congressional and senate campaigns had few political items. The "Me and Roosevelt for Johnson" button from 1941 and the "Blanco County Ladies for Lyndon" are two of the most popular buttons in the hobby.

1. "Me and Roosevelt for Johnson" is the most sought-after LBJ button. In the 1941 special election, Johnson emphasized his close relationship with FDR but still lost to Pappy O'Daniel. Jack Wilson Collection.

2. A cigarette lighter and matches were popular giveaways until smoking began to be politically incorrect.

3. "Blanco County Ladies for Lyndon" is quite rare. Jack Wilson Collection.

4. "Johnson for '68" was Johnson's last button, as he decided not to run for re-election in March of that year.

SUPPORT ROOSEVELT AND JOHNSON

Won't you help?
Your country,
yourself and
your good friend.
Elect

**Lyndon Johnson
U. S. Senator**

Lyndon Johnson and Farmer Friend

ME and ROOSEVELT FOR JOHNSON

1

JOHNSON FOR '68

4

SEN. JOHNSON DINNER

LADIES FOR LYNDON

Blanco County

3

Lyndon Johnson
MAJORITY LEADER
US SENATE

2

ROOSEVELT and UNITY

LYNDON JOHNSON

● EXPERIENCED ●
● DEPENDABLE ●

My dear ...Charles...:

My friend, Congressman Lyndon Johnson, is a candidate for election to the Senate, June 28. Texas needs the energy, good judgment, and extraordinary productive capacity for which he is well-known. His record for achievement as a Congressman is unmatched. He has worked tirelessly for all Texans—the farmer, the laboring man, the young, the aged. In emergency times when national defense problems must be faced squarely, we need a man of his qualifications and experience in the Senate.

I will consider it a personal favor, and I believe you will be doing a public service if you will use your influence in the interest of his candidacy.

Sincerely your friend,

ELECT LYNDON JOHNSON YOUR United States SENATOR

1

6

6

LBJ **FOR** **USA**

TEXAS YD's

4

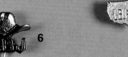

6

JOHNSON HUMPHREY

LEADERS OF OUR COUNTRY

KENNEDY & JOHNSON

AND A FRIENDLY WORLD

44th INAUGURATION

1961

The New Frontier

5

6

6

JOHNSON·HUMPHREY

VOTE DEMOCRATIC

2

JOHNSON·HUMPHREY

VOTE DEMOCRATIC

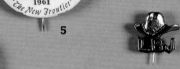

NEW LEADERSHIP

KENNEDY JOHNSON

3

6

LBJ 6

KENNEDY **JOHNSON**

Ticket for Texans!

PLATE 2

Lyndon Johnson

1. This is a bolo-tie clasp made out of plastic.

2. On close inspection, two seemingly identical buttons show Johnson larger in one, Humphrey larger in the other. The story goes that Johnson was unhappy with the button showing a large Humphrey, so a second group of buttons were made, correcting this obvious oversight.

3. This is the button that started my collection and interest in politics.

4. This presidential bumper sticker was produced by the Texas Young Democrats, a group comprised primarily of college students who were active in Texas for many years.

5. Inaugural buttons began with George Washington. A "jugate" shows both candidates on the same button.

6. Johnson's campaign had numerous small pins and jewelry made for the election. Shown is just an example of the variety of available pieces.

PLATE 3

Lyndon Johnson

1. The LBJ brand and the Stetson left no doubt as to the identity and home state of the candidate.

2. The Johnson campaign reached out to youth groups, as seen in this Young Texans button and the "Young Citizens for Johnson-Humphrey" card.

3. Lady Bird Johnson campaigned by train, plane, and automobile for her husband.

4. An always-popular yellow rose ribbon.

IT'S NOT LUCK THAT RULES THE NATION
it's the MAN vote
JOHNSON

JOHNSON HUMPHREY
VOTE DEMOCRAT

I USED TO BE A REPUBLICAN
vote LBJ

LET'S BACK JOHNSON

YOUNG TEXANS FOR JOHNSON
2

WELCOME LADYBIRD FLYING WHISTLESTOP
3

TEXANS for JOHNSON
4

ALL THE WAY WITH LBJ VOTE DEMOCRATIC
1

JOHNSON for PRESIDENT

Young Citizens For JOHNSON-HUMPHREY 4 FOR 64
Member
Chuck Bailey
Texas High School Division
State Co-Chairman
2

Vote For President
George Bush.

The Future of America
in the Hands of Experience.
President George Bush.

TEXANS FOR
WE WANT
ROPERS
NOT
DOPERS!
BUSH★QUAYLE '92

Kids
FOR
BUSH
© O. Ltd. 1988

GEORGE BUSH
PRESIDENT 1980

JAN 20,1981
REAGAN
BUSH
Texas
Was There!

1

VIVA
BUSH!
RNHA

TEXANS
FOR
BUSH

George
BUSH
88

1984 REPUBLICAN NATIONAL CONVENTION
REAGAN
BUSH'84
VIVA! TEXAS OLE!
2

BUSH★'92

BUSH
★★★
QUAYLE
'92

1992
GOP
3

Another Perot Volunteer For
BUSH★
4

PLATE 4

George H. W. Bush

George H. W. Bush served as the forty-first president of the United States. In the late 1940s, he moved his family to Midland and later to Houston where he was elected to the U.S. House of Representatives. In 1964, he ran unsuccessfully for U.S. Senate against incumbent Ralph Yarborough. In 1970, he lost a U.S. Senate race to Lloyd Bentsen. After service as chairman of the Republican National Committee and ambassador to the U.N. and China, he ran for president in 1980. He joined the Reagan team as vice president, served two terms, and won the election for president in 1988. He lost to Bill Clinton in 1992 and returned to Houston. He is the father of George W. Bush, the forty-third president of the United States, and of Jeb Bush, the governor of Florida. His father was a U.S. senator from Connecticut.

1. President Bush flew a torpedo bomber in WWII. The gold-tone lapel pin is designed to look like one of those planes.

2. Texas delegation button to the 1984 Republican National Convention.

3. Here Bush and his vice president, Dan Quayle, are pictured in the elephant's ears. This style of button has been used in several campaigns.

4. Ross Perot, an independent candidate for president, was known to have rabid volunteers. With this bumper sticker, the Bush campaign was tapping into that energy.

PLATE 5

George H. W. Bush

1, 2. Bush Belles were a group of female supporters in the 1970 senate race.

GEORGE BUSH
For United States Senator

A.D.L.U.550

GEORGE BUSH
For United States Senator
He can do more.

BUSH
belles

1

I'M FOR
BUSH

ELECT GEORGE
BUSH
REPUBLICAN FOR
U. S. SENATE

2

GEORGE
BUSH

WE
NEED
GEORGE
BUSH
IN U.S.
SENATE

BUSH

Something you can
hold on to.

Bush
George W. Bush for Congress

Bush

2

George BUSH

3

995 TEXAS INAUGURAL

4

Governor Bush
Responsibility ⭐ Opportunity
for our Future

RESPONSIBILITY AND OPPORTUNITY FOR THE FUTURE OF TEXAS.

"I want to continue as Governor to build on the reforms of the last four years. I have done in office what I said I'd do. We've laid a strong foundation. Now it's time to build."

REPUBLICAN STATE CONVENTION
JUNE 13-14, 1998
FORT WORTH, TEXAS

George W.
Bush
For Texas Governor
ELECTION NIGHT VICTORY PARTY
November 8, 1994
I WAS THERE!
AUSTIN, TEXAS

5

George W.
Bush
For Texas Governor

6

Bush Texas
Governor

Pol. ad paid for by Gov. Bush Committee, 807 Brazos, Suite 800, Austin, TX 78701

PLATE 6

George W. Bush

George W. Bush, the son of a president and grandson of a U.S. senator, first ran for office in 1978, losing a U.S. congressional race to Democrat Kent Hance. In 1994, he defeated incumbent Ann Richards in a hotly contested gubernatorial race. He was re-elected governor in 1998 and in 2000 was elected president. He was re-elected in 2004.

1, 2, 3. A palm card and two buttons from Bush's losing race in 1978.

4. A pocketknife commemorating the 1995 inauguration as governor of Texas.

5. A 1994 "Ranger" badge, complete with cut-out star. Bush continued to use these kinds of pins in his presidential races.

6. This button was issued for the Texas primary race in 1998.

PLATE 7

George W. Bush

1. The Black Tie and Boots Inaugural Ball is one of the most popular of the inaugural parties. This was especially so in 2001, with a Texan headed for the White House.

2. Bush was the general partner in a group that owned the Texas Rangers baseball team.

3. "Frogs for Bush!": TCU button from the 2004 Republican National Convention.

4. In the 2000 presidential race, George Bush became better known as "W." Many buttons play on that theme.

2001 BLACK TIE & BOOTS INAUGURAL BALL

TEXAS STATE SOCIETY OF WASHINGTON, DC

CLINT BLACK & LISA HARTMAN

TANYA TUCKER

Other performers:
☆ The Beach Boys ☆ Asleep at the Wheel ☆
☆ Mark Chesnutt ☆ Lee Greenwood ☆

FRIDAY, JANUARY 19, 2001

1

W
is for
Women

2000

BUSH   CHENEY

GOP

W ☆**'04**

4

TEXAS RANGER FAN

FOR BUSH

2

W

W

FROGS
for
Bush!
TCU REPUBLICANS
FT. WORTH, TX

3

W.

STANDS FOR
Whuppin!

W.
is for
Winner!

2004

TEXAS DELEGATION

Republican National Convention

July 31- Aug 3, 2000 Philadelphia, PA

2

VIVA BUSH

1

ELECTION NIGHT VICTORY 2000

GEORGE W. BUSH FOR PRESIDENT

MARCH 14 - AUSTIN, TEXAS

3

BUSH 2000 CHENEY

GEORGE W. BUSH

BUSH CHENEY '04

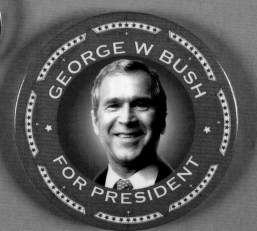

GEORGE W BUSH FOR PRESIDENT

PLATE 8

George W. Bush

1. The "Viva Bush" slogan was used to woo the increasingly important Hispanic vote.

2. The Texas delegation button for the 2000 Republican National Convention.

3. The election night party was held, but the victory had to wait for a Supreme Court decision regarding the Florida election.

PLATE 9

U.S. Senate

The first U.S. senators from Texas were Sam Houston and Thomas J. Rusk. The Houston succession was filled by such senators as Richard Coke, Joseph Weldon Bailey, Morris Sheppard, Houston's son Andrew Jackson Houston, W. Lee O'Daniel, Lyndon Johnson, John Tower, and Phil Gramm. It is now held by John Cornyn. The Rusk succession included John H. Reagan, Charles Culberson, Tom Connally, Price Daniel, Ralph Yarborough, and Lloyd Bentsen. It is now held by Kay Bailey Hutchison.

1. Price Daniel served as Speaker of the Texas House, attorney general, governor, U.S. senator, and associate justice of the Texas Supreme Court.

2. Jim Hart, of Austin, ran for the Senate in the 1957 special election. He also served as an associate justice on the Texas Supreme Court.

3. Gordon McClendon, "The Old Scotchman," was a radio and sports announcer. He ran for the Senate in the 1966 primary but lost.

4. An "Alvin Owsley for Senate" thimble. He ran and lost in 1928 but was famous for his heroics in WWI and for serving as minister to Romania under FDR.

5. The son of a San Antonio mayor and congressman, Maury Maverick, Jr., ran for the Senate in the 1961 special election to replace Lyndon Johnson.

6. Jack Porter was the Republican candidate running against Lyndon Johnson in the 1948 general election.

7. A former Dallas district attorney, associate justice of the Texas Supreme Court, and attorney general of Texas, Will Wilson lost this race for the U.S. Senate. As attorney general he shut down the gambling industry in Galveston.

8. Bill Blakley, a Dallas lawyer and businessman, was appointed twice to the U.S. Senate. In 1957 he was appointed to replace Price Daniel and in 1961 to replace Lyndon Johnson. He lost both races for the unexpired term. He is the only man to hold the senate seats in both the Houston and Rusk successions.

9. Thad Hutcheson, a Houston Republican, ran for the Senate in 1956.

10. Martin Dies, a Democratic congressman from southeast Texas, lost this senate race in the special election of 1961. He was best known for his anti-communist hearings as chairman of the House Committee on Un-American Activities. He served in the House from 1931–1945 and from 1953–1959.

The Story of

BILL BLAKLEY

LAWYER - RANCHER - BUSINESSMAN

Candidate For

UNITED STATES SENATOR

8

Texas Needs a

maverick

in the Senate

Special Election April 4, 1961

5

5

THAD

9

VIVA
BLAKLEY
DEMOCRAT

8

Jim

2

THE OLD SCOTCHMAN
GORDON
McLENDON
DEMOCRAT
FOR
U.S. SENATE

3

I'M VOTING
BLAKLEY
DEMOCRAT

8

ELECT
"THE OLD SCOTCHMAN"
McLENDON
GORDON
DEMOCRAT
FOR
U.S. SENATE

3

PRICE
DANIEL
FOR
U.S. SENATOR

1

JACK
PORTER
FOR U.S.
SENATOR

6

I'M FOR
MARTIN
DIES
FOR
U.S. SENATOR

10

STRENGTH

for Texas

Will Wilson

for

UNITED STATES
SENATOR

7

I'm
for
WILL
WILSON

7

4

Strohmeyer & Wyman, Publishers, New York, N.Y.

Sold only by Underwood & Underwood New York, London, Toronto, Canada, Ottawa, Kansas

Hon. Joseph W. Bailey, Member of Congress from Texas.
Copyright 1899 by Strohmeyer & Wyman.

4

JOSEPH WELDON BAILEY

4

JAKE WOLTERS A DEMOCRAT

2

FOR SENATOR CHOICE B. RANDELL

1

FOR U. S. SENATOR Ex-Gov. O. B. COLQUITT

7

TOM CONNALLY FOR SENATE

6

FOR U. S. SENATOR EARLE B. MAYFIELD

8

MORRIS SHEPPARD FOR SENATOR

3

Jos. W. Bailey, Jr.

Candidate for

United States SENATOR

Subject to the Action of the Democratic Primaries

45

5

JOSEPH W. BAILEY, JR. FOR SENATOR

5

5

Jos. W. BAILEY, JR. for SENATOR

9

184

5

PLATE 10

U.S. Senate

1. Choice Randell ran for the Senate in 1912. He served as "Congressman from Sherman."

2. Jake Wolters, a Democrat from Fayette and Harris Counties, lost in the 1912 primary. He was an anti-prohibitionist leader.

3. Morris Sheppard served as U.S. senator from 1913 to 1941.

4. Joseph W. Bailey served in the U.S. House, and from 1901 to 1913 he served in the U.S. Senate. His political career ended in scandal related to questionable payments made to him from the oil industry.

5. Joseph W. Bailey, Jr., followed his father into politics, running for the U.S. Senate in 1934. He lost to Tom Connally.

6. Tom Connally served in the U.S. Senate from 1929 to 1953.

7. O. B. Colquitt made an unsuccessful run for the U.S. Senate in 1916. *Jack Wilson Collection.*

8. Earle B. Mayfield, the KKK-supported candidate, served as U.S. senator from 1922 to 1928. *Jack Wilson Collection.*

PLATE 11

U.S. Senate

1. Former Cowboys quarterback Roger Staubach was frequently mentioned as a candidate in 1980.

2. Republican Beau Boulter, from Amarillo, made fun of a Lloyd Bentsen breakfast fund-raiser for Washington lobbyists.

3. John Cornyn was elected to the U.S. Senate in 2004 after serving on the Texas Supreme Court and as state attorney general.

4. State senator and former Fort Worth mayor Hugh Parmer ran for the Senate in 1990.

5. Democrat Victor Morales, a schoolteacher from Crandall, Texas, toured Texas in an old pickup. Surprisingly, the heretofore political unknown would claim the Democratic nomination in 1996.

6. A former congressman from Dallas, Jim Collins ran for the U.S. Senate in 1982.

7. After serving two terms as Texas attorney general, Jim Mattox lost a race for the Senate in 1994.

8. Jose Angel Gutierrez, a founder of La Raza Unida, ran as a Democrat in 1992.

9. Richard Fisher, a Dallas businessman, won the Democratic nomination in 1994 only to lose to Kay Bailey Hutchison.

10. Democrat Bob Krueger, a Shakespeare scholar and congressman from New Braunfels, ran unsuccessfully for the U.S. Senate in 1978 and 1984. He was appointed to the Senate by Ann Richards in 1993. He was defeated by Kay Bailey Hutchison in the June 1993 special election for the unexpired term of retiring Lloyd Bentsen. He later served as ambassador to Burundi and Botswana.

11. Lloyd Doggett lost the 1984 U.S. Senate race to Phil Gramm. He served his hometown of Austin as state senator and now serves as U.S. congressman.

Draft
Staubach
U.S. Senate

1

BOULTER
BREAKFAST
CLUB

2

Senator Hugh
PARMER
FOR U. S. SENATE

Paid for by the Senator Parmer Committee
Capitol Station, P. O. Box 12007, Austin, TX 78711
Harold Hammett, Treasurer.

4

Jim Mattox

DEMOCRAT for U.S. SENATE
• TOUGH
• FAIR
• CONSISTENT

7

KRUEGER
OF TEXAS

10

Women
for
Cornyn

www.johncornyn.com
Paid for by John Cornyn for Senate, Inc.

3

For United States Senate

Victor Morales

5

Richard Fisher
UP & AWAY TO VICTORY IN '94
U. S. Senator - Texas

9

Cornyn ★ ★ ★
★ ★ *for*
Senate

3

COLLINS
U.S.
SENATE

PAID FOR BY FRIENDS OF JIM COLLINS

6

JOSE ANGEL GUTIERREZ

Democrat • U.S. Senate

Paid for by the Gutiérrez Senate Campaign • Anne Vincent, Treasurer
235-A West 12th Street, Dallas, Texas 75208

8

Yellow
Doggett
Democrat

11

1

ELECT
RALPH YARBOROUGH
for your
GOVERNOR

Judge . Lawyer . Veteran . Statesman
46

TEXAS
YARBOROUGH
PROGRESS

4

RWY

5

Y

6

Re-elect
Yarborough
Senator

RE-ELECT
U.S. SENATOR
RALPH W.
YARBOROUGH
DEMOCRAT
THE PEOPLE'S SENATOR

3

☆ Southwest Conference ☆
FOOTBALL SCHEDULE

☆   ☆   ☆   Courtesy of   ☆   ☆   ☆

RALPH YARBOROUGH
United States Senator

2

¡Viva!
Yarborough
'72

Youth for
Yarborough
'72

6

Yarborough
72

RE-ELECT RALPH
YARBOROUGH

YARBOROUGH

PLATE 12

Ralph Yarborough

alph Yarborough served Texas as an assistant attorney general under Jimmy Allred, as a Travis County district judge, and as a U.S. senator. His campaigns against Allan Shivers were among the nastiest campaigns in Texas history. Yarborough ran for governor in 1952, 1954, and 1956, barely losing in runoffs to Shivers and Price Daniel. In 1957, he ran in a special U.S. Senate campaign and served in the Senate until 1971.

1. "Yarborough for Governor" stamps.

2. A Southwest Conference schedule in the days when the now-extinct Southwest Conference was made up of Texas and Arkansas schools.

3. Yarborough wooden nickel.

4. From Yarborough's 1950s campaigns.

5. Yarborough's metal yellow rose lapel pin is one of the most attractive pins in the collection.

6. "Youth for Yarborough" buttons.

PLATE 13

Phil Gramm

Phil Gramm, a Texas A&M professor, was elected as a Democrat to the U.S. Congress in the late 1970s. In 1982, he resigned from Congress and switched his affiliation to the Republican Party. He won re-election to Congress in a special election and was elected to the U.S. Senate in 1984. In 1996, he made an unsuccessful bid for the Republican presidential nomination. He left office in 2000.

1. This is probably a congressional button.

2. "Reagan & Gramm": Gramm used these "coattail" buttons in Texas to good effect.

GRAMM COUNTRY '96

ASK ME ABOUT PHIL GRAMM

1

RE-ELECT For Senator 1996 PHIL GRAMM

Phil Gramm
my Senator

'96 GRAMM PRESIDENT

OFFICIAL GRAMM WAGON PULLER

2

GRAMM
U.S. Senate

FOR AMERICA
FOR TEXAS

FOR TEXAS ★ FOR AMERICA
REAGAN & GRAMM

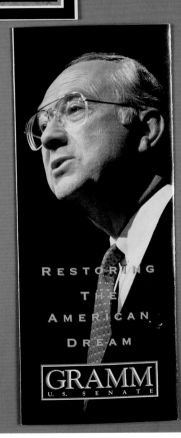
RESTORING THE AMERICAN DREAM
GRAMM
U.S. SENATE

bentsen.
FOR
president

BENTSEN IN '76 COMMITTEE • CHAIRMAN: William Lane • TREASURER: Shannon H. Ratliff

BOSTON to AUSTIN
19 88
DUKAKIS-BENTSEN

BENTSEN
VICE PRESIDENT
in '88

BENTSEN
IN 76

ΨΗΦΙΣΕΤΕ
ΒΕΝΤΣΕΝ
ΓΙΑ
ΠΡΟΕΔΡΟ

1

Dukakis
Bentsen
Paid for by Grayson County Young Democrats

DUKAKIS
PRESIDENT '88
BENTSEN
VICE PRESIDENT '88

ELECT
BENTSEN
PRESIDENT

DUKAKIS BENTSEN
'88
FROST

2

bentsen

PLATE 14

Lloyd Bentsen

loyd Bentsen was elected to the U.S. Senate in 1970 after defeating incumbent Ralph Yarborough in the Democratic primary and George H. W. Bush in the general election. He ran for president in the 1976 primary and was Michael Dukakis's running mate in the 1988 presidential election.

1. Button in Greek used in both the 1976 presidential and senate campaigns. Although Texas law allows a name to be on a ballot only one time, the "LBJ exemption" allows a presidential or vice presidential candidate also to run for the U.S. Senate from Texas. The exemption was first used by Johnson in 1960 when he simultaneously ran for re-election to the Senate and for the office of vice president.

2. This is a coattail button, whereby a lesser candidate hopes to find success by riding a presidential team's coattails. Martin Frost won his congressional race despite the short coattails of Dukakis and Bentsen.

PLATE 15

Lloyd Bentsen

1. "Senator for the Seventies" was used in Bentsen's first campaign for the Senate in 1970.

2. These buttons were used in both the presidential and senatorial campaigns.

**Bentsen.
Senator
for the
Seventies.**

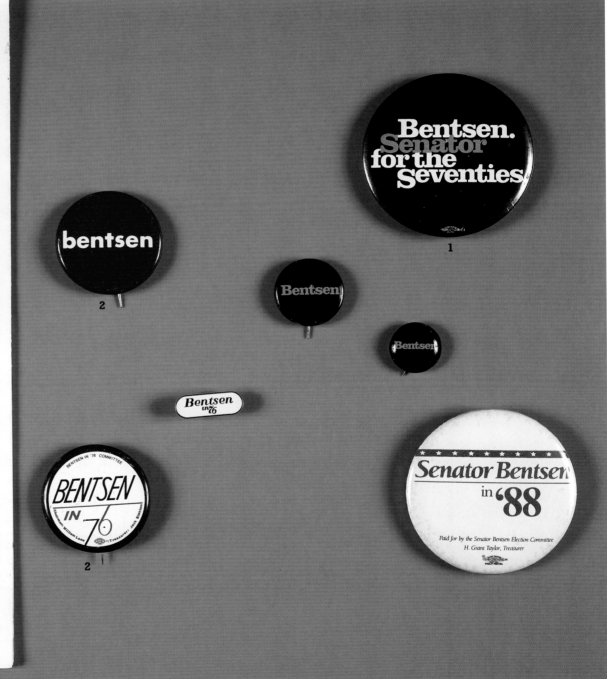

Kay Bailey **HUTCHISON** ★ ★ ★ ★ ★
★ ★ *State Treasurer*

Pol. Adv. Pd. for by Friends of Kay Hutchison, Bob Drieger, Treasurer, 1900 First City Center, Dallas, TX 75201.

Kay Bailey Hutchison

FOR
U.S. SENATOR
ELECT
KAY BAILEY HUTCHISON

AM PRODUCTIONS AUSTIN, TEXAS 800-572-0705 PAID FOR BY KAY BAILEY HUTCHISON SENATOR COMMITTEE

PLATE 16

Kay Bailey Hutchison

The first woman from Texas to serve in the U.S. Senate, Kay Bailey Hutchison previously served in the Texas House and as state treasurer. Among her campaign items are scarves, clips, luggage tags, and a magnifying glass.

PLATE 17

John Tower

John Tower, a Republican professor from Wichita Falls, ran for the U.S. Senate in 1960 against Lyndon Johnson. Because Johnson won both his old Senate seat and the vice presidency, he resigned from the Senate, and Tower won the seat in a special election in 1961. Tower was elected again in 1966, 1972, and 1978. He left office in 1984. In 1991 he was killed in a plane crash.

1. This is a fancy tie tack, probably given to big supporters.

2. Tower chewing gum.

3. A "coattail" button from 1972: John Tower for Senate, Richard Nixon for president, and Hank Grover, of Houston, for governor.

4. An unusual psychedelic brochure from the 1972 campaign.

"I stand for Texas in the U.S. Senate"

John Tower
Always has. Always will.

STICK WITH *John Tower*
HE STANDS FOR TEXAS.

2

John Tower
He stands for Texas.

TOWER
NIXON
GROVER

3

'this is a pam-phlet for →

4

OUR TOWER
Favorite!

Tower

1

TOWER
TEXAS
72

TOWER FOR U.S. SENATOR ADLU550

RE-ELECT RE-ELECT RE-ELECT RE-ELECT RE-ELECT
TOWER TOWER TOWER TOWER TOWER
RE-ELECT RE-ELECT RE-ELECT RE-ELECT RE-ELECT

TOWER TOWER TOWER TOWER TOWER

1

TOWER

TOWER

2

TOWER

JOHN TOWER FOR PRESIDENT

TOWER FOR V.P.

TOWER

John Tower
U.S. SENATOR

"Paid for and authorized by Texans for Tower, John F. Davis, III, Treasurer". A copy of our report is filed with the Federal Election Commission and is available for purchase from the Federal Election Commission, Washington, D.C. If you are a federal employee, please disregard this request.

RE-ELECT SENATOR JOHN TOWER

KEEP TOWER

PLATE 18

John Tower

1. A book of Tower stamps.

2. An early Tower button for his 1960 campaign. It was the same design used by Richard Nixon in his 1960 presidential campaign in Texas.

PLATE 19

Texans in Congress

Texas members of Congress have wielded power in Washington for many years. Inclined to leave its members in place for decades, Texas was a force to be reckoned with while the old seniority rules were in place. After those rules were relaxed, Texas maintained its influence through party leadership rules. Three Texans have served as Speaker, and Texans have held many important leadership positions and chairmanships over the years.

1. Wright Patman, from Texarkana, served as chairman of the powerful House Committee on Banking and Currency from 1963 to 1975. Patman served in Congress from 1929 to 1976.

2. A. P. Barrett and H. A. Wood are portrayed in a cello button and a metal shirt stud. While both of these items are thought to be from Texas, they are illustrative of the difficulty in identifying certain politicians. A. P. Barrett was also a state senator from Bonham, and H. A. Wood ran as a Progressive in 1898.

3. A great rebus for Bob Eckhart, from Harris County.

4. An early tobacco trade card for future Senator Joseph Bailey.

5. Jim Collins, a Dallas Republican, served in Congress and ran for the U.S. Senate and for mayor of Dallas.

6. George Mahon, from Lubbock, was another long-tenured congressman, serving from 1935 to 1978. He acted as chair of the House Committee on Appropriations from 1964 until he retired in 1978.

7. Maury Maverick, Sr., from San Antonio, served in Congress from 1935 to 1938, a seat he won as a staunch New Deal congressman. He was mayor of San Antonio from 1939 to 1941.

8. W. R. Bob Poage of Waco served from 1937 to 1978. The "farmers' friend," he chaired the House Agriculture Committee from 1967 to 1974.

9. Bill Kilgarlin, a Houston Democrat, later served on the Texas Supreme Court.

10. The Boll Weevils were a group of Southern Democratic congressmen who often voted with the Republicans during the Reagan years.

11. Graham Purcell, from Wichita Falls, served in Congress from 1963 to 1972.

12. Dale Milford went from television weatherman in Dallas to congressman in 1973. The native of Bug Tussle in Fannin County served until 1979.

13. Ron Paul, MD, has served in Congress both as a Republican and a Libertarian. He was the Libertarian candidate for president in 1988. Candidates often use family recipes for campaign items.

WRIGHT PATMAN
for CONGRESS
(RE-ELECTION)

1

FOR CONGRESS
A. P. BARRETT

2

2

RE-ELECT
MAVERICK

374

7

HE WORKS FOR US
PURCELL
PEOPLE
WE WORK FOR HIM

11

THIS IS A
PAID POLITICAL AD
PAID FOR BY
DALE MILFORD
207 W. MAIN, GRAND PRAIRIE
TEXAS 75050 — PRINTED BY
DAVIS & STANTON, 4340
N. CENTRAL EXPRESSWAY
DALLAS, TEXAS
75206

12

EK

3

George Mahon
FOR CONGRESS

JOIN COLLINS Now!

5

Hon. Jos. W. Bailey,
U.S. Rep. from Texas.

4

6

Re-elect
POAGE
FOR
CONGRESS

8

I'M FOR
KILGARLIN
FOR CONGRESS!

9

BOLL WEEVIL

10

The
Ron Paul Family

Congressman & Mrs. Ron Paul

COOKBOOK

13

Keep **Tiger Teague**

He fights fair.
He works hard.
He gets things done.

Tiger Teague
U.S. CONGRESS - SIXTH DISTRICT
Vote Tuesday, Nov. 2

Paid for and authorized by Teague for Congress Committee
Dr. James R. Gill, Treasurer

1

Jack
BROOKS
FOR CONGRESS

3

9

4

DALLAS NEEDS
CABELL
FOR CONGRESS

2

Re-Elect
O.C. FISHER
CONGRESSMAN

6

DEE-DAY
NOV. 8th 1966
DEE MILLER
FOR CONGRESS

5

LET'S KEEP
BOB CASEY

8

"KEEP COOL WITH POOL"
RE-ELECT
JOE POOL
CONGRESSMAN AT LARGE
2nd TERM

7

FIGHTING FOR
ALGER
AMERICA

10

Kika

11

PLATE 20

Texans in Congress

1. Olin Earl "Tiger" Teague from College Station served in Congress from 1946 to 1978. The second-most-decorated soldier in WWII (after fellow Texan Audie Murphy), he served on the Committee on Veterans' Affairs, chairing it from 1955 to 1972.

2. Earl Cabell, a former Dallas mayor, was elected to Congress in 1965 and served until 1973.

3. Jack Brooks of Beaumont served in Congress from 1952 to 1995. Like other long-serving Texans, he was a chairman of the powerful House Judiciary Committee. A famous picture shows him standing next to Lyndon Johnson on Air Force One as Johnson is sworn in as president following President Kennedy's assassination.

4. Jack Hightower served in the Texas House of Representatives, the Texas Senate, the U.S. Congress, and the Texas Supreme Court. He has one of the most outstanding collections of signed political books in the country.

5. Dee Miller, from Amarillo, was celebrating a special day in 1966 but failed to win a seat in Congress.

6. O. C. Fisher, congressman and historian, represented San Angelo from 1942 to 1974.

7. Before the U.S. Supreme Court's "one man, one vote" ruling, Texas had a congressman-at-large elected statewide. This fan kept Joe Pool's constituents cool from 1963 to 1968.

8. Bob Casey, from Houston, served in Congress from 1959 to 1976, when he became a commissioner of the Federal Maritime Commission.

9. "All for Hall from Rockwall": a congressional lucky penny used by Ralph Hall.

10. Bruce Alger was a Republican congressman for Dallas who served from 1955 to 1965.

11. Democrat Eligio "Kika" de la Garza from Mercedes served in Congress from 1965 to 1997.

PLATE 21

Texas Congress

1. Lloyd Doggett, a former state senator, U.S. Senate candidate, and Texas Supreme Court justice, has served Austin in Congress since 1995.

2. Charles Stenholm, a conservative West Texas Democrat, served in Congress from 1979 to 2004.

3. In the summer of 2004, a special session of the Texas Legislature dedicated to congressional redistricting re-drew the districts of the five incumbents pictured on this button. In the 2005 election, only Chet Edwards of Waco survived.

4. Often given credit for the redistricting defeat of the "Texas Five," former House Majority Leader Tom DeLay served as a Republican from Sugar Land and resigned in 2006.

5. Lamar Smith, who represents a large swath of central and southwest Texas, has served in Congress since 1987.

6. Dick Armey, a University of North Texas professor, was elected to Congress in 1985. He served as House majority leader from 1994 until his retirement in 2002.

7. Martin Frost, a Democrat from the Fort Worth area, served as chair of the House Democratic Committee until he lost his seat, primarily due to the 2003 redistricting effort.

8. Jim Wright, mayor of Weatherford, congressman, and Democratic majority leader and Speaker of the House (1987–1990), served in Congress from 1955 to 1989. He made an unsuccessful run for the U.S. Senate in the 1961 special election. He currently lives in Fort Worth.

LLOYD
DOGGETT
1996
10th
DISTRICT
for
CONGRESS

1

STENHOLM
17th
DIST.
TEXAS
Democrat - U.S. Congress

2

I'm
Voting
WRIGHT!
FOR CONGRESS

8

I SUPPORT THE
TEXAS 5
★ CHET EDWARDS
★ MARTIN FROST
★ NICK LAMPSON
★ MAX SANDLIN
★ CHARLIE STENHOLM

3

DeLAY
U.S. CONGRESS
PAID FOR BY TOM DeLAY FOR CONGRESS COMMITTEE

4

WRIGHT
for
80

KEEP
WRIGHT
WORKING FOR US

FROST
DEMOCRAT
U.S. CONGRESS

7

DICK
ARMEY
1996
26th
DISTRICT
for
CONGRESS

6

Lamar
Smith

5

I ♥
Jim Wright

FOR
SENATOR
WRIGHT
IS
RIGHT

Texas Democrats Salute
JIM WRIGHT
50

GARNER

GARNER FOR President

JOHN GARNER FOR PRESIDENT

JOHN GARNER FOR PRESIDENT

JOHN NANCE GARNER
SPEAKER OF THE HOUSE

GARNER FOR PRESIDENT
TEXAS

3

GARNER FOR PRESIDENT

GREEN DUCK CHICAGO
GARNER

UVALDE, TEXAS
The Home of VICE PRESIDENT
JOHN NANCE GARNER

The GARNER GAVELS in our Lobby

KINCAID HOTEL
UVALDE, TEXAS

GARNER FARLEY BANQUET
STATE DEMOCRATIC EXECUTIVE COMMITTEE
Oct. 19, 1933
Dallas

2

1933

1

ROOSEVELT and GARNER

PLATE 22

John Nance Garner

John Nance "Cactus Jack" Garner served Texas in Congress from 1903 to 1933 and was elected Speaker of the House in 1931. He was Franklin Roosevelt's vice president until Roosevelt's third run in 1940. Garner took on his former running mate, lost, and retired to Uvalde. "Cactus Jack" lived into his nineties, and his remark that the vice president's job wasn't "worth a bucket of warm spit" is still often quoted.

1. A colorful ticket from the 1933 inauguration.

2. A ribbon celebrating a 1933 Dallas banquet for Garner and Postmaster General James Farley.

3. Garner was a serious presidential candidate before joining the Roosevelt ticket.

PLATE 23

Jake Pickle

A consummate politician, Jake Pickle of Austin was elected to represent Lyndon Johnson's old district from 1963 until his retirement in 1999. He always had a pocketful of pickle pins and squeaking toy pickles.

1. "Jake" plastic pickle pins were the type of memorabilia that his constituents would keep forever. They will be turning up in jewelry boxes and drawers for years to come.

2. A picture was taken showing a crowd at a Pickle gathering wearing these masks. It was disconcerting to say the least.

3. Pickle was never without these squeaky plastic pickles.

4. Only in Texas: Jake Pickle dominoes. Campaign dominoes were also used by several other Texas congressmen, including Marvin Leath, Joe Barton, Charles Stenholm, and Charlie Wilson.

5. Squeeze the miniature flashlight for Pickle light.

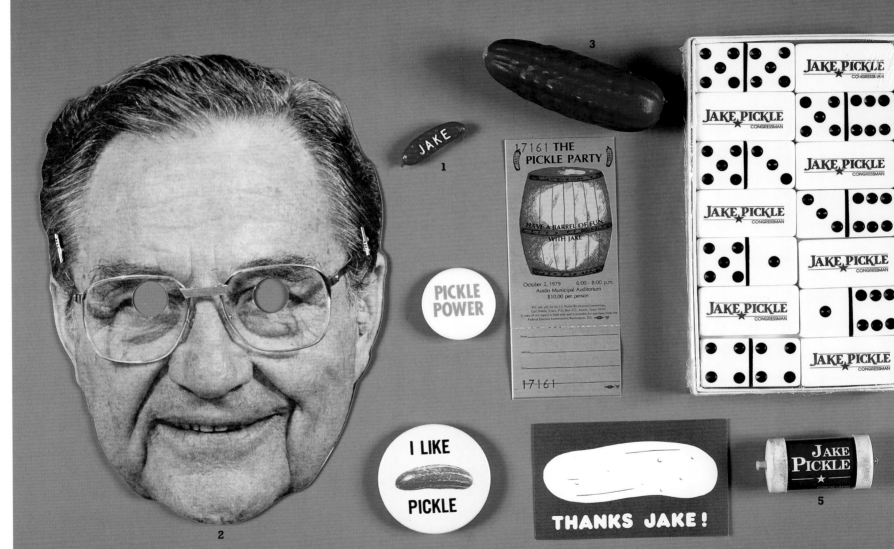

1

JAKE

2

3

17161 THE
PICKLE PARTY

HAVE A BARREL OF FUN
WITH JAKE

October 2, 1979   6:00 - 8:00 p.m.
Austin Municipal Auditorium
$10.00 per person

Pol. adv. pd. for by J.J. Pickle Re-election Committee,
Carl Hobbs, Treas., P.O. Box 717, Austin, Texas 78767
A copy of our report is filed with and is available for purchase from the
Federal Election Commission, Washington, D.C.

Name

Address

City

17161

PICKLE
POWER

JAKE PICKLE
CONGRESSMAN

JAKE PICKLE
CONGRESSMAN

JAKE PICKLE
CONGRESSMAN

JAKE PICKLE
CONGRESSMAN

JAKE PICKLE
CONGRESSMAN

JAKE PICKLE
CONGRESSMAN

4

I LIKE

PICKLE

THANKS JAKE!

JAKE
PICKLE
CONGRESSMAN

5

THE AYES OF TEXAS ARE ON **NIXON**

1960 — Nov. 8. Election day

1

TEXAS P
FOR
HOOVER

4

ROOSEVELT
GARNER
BULLINGTON

7

COMPLIMENTS OF
CONNELL, BROS. & CO.,
DEALERS IN
Dry Goods, Clothing, Boots & Shoes,
AND RANCH SUPPLIES,
Sweetwater, Texas.

GROVER CLEVELAND

10

Texans
for
McGovern
Shriver

5

MIDLAND
WELCOMES
**PRESIDENT
FORD**

8

TEXAS
IS
WALLACE
COUNTRY

2

TEXAS
FOR
TAFT

6

WILLKIE
AND
McNARY

DELEGATE
—
Texas State
Republican
Convention
BEAUMONT
Aug. 13, 1940

9

Howard
Dean
Democrat for President
www.DeanForTexas.com

11

JESSE JACKSON
88
TEXAS

3

PRESIDENTS IN
LONGVIEW, TEXAS · JAN. 30, 1936

13

TUCKER-GOETTINGER
NRA
WE DO OUR PART

12

PLATE 24

Presidential Elections and Texas

From its earliest days, Texas has been important to presidential candidates. During the years when Texas was an independent republic (1836–1845), U.S. presidential candidates ran for and against bringing Texas into the Union. After annexation, as early as 1856, Texas Senator Sam Houston was considered a possible presidential contender. Since then, John Nance Garner, Lyndon Johnson, George H. W. Bush, George W. Bush, Phil Gramm, Lloyd Bentsen, Ross Perot, John Connally, and Ron Paul have run for the presidency. The variety of "Texans for _____" (write in your choice) buttons and ribbons shows that the parties and candidates consider Texas's population and money of paramount importance.

1. Postcard from Richard Nixon's 1960 campaign. He is shown in his famous kitchen debate with Soviet Premier Nikita Kruschev.

2. George Wallace made strong runs in Texas in 1968 and 1972.

3. Jessie Jackson brought his Rainbow Coalition to Texas.

4. Herbert Hoover did not give up on the "solid South" and Texas.

5. This button is from George McGovern's Harris County headquarters in 1972.

6. This is probably from Robert Taft's campaign in 1956.

7. Even Republican gubernatorial candidate Orville Bullington linked his campaign with the Roosevelt-Garner ticket in 1932.

8. President Ford campaigned in Midland, home of future president George W. Bush.

9. A Willkie supporter attended the state Republican Convention in Beaumont in 1940.

10. A Sweetwater dry goods store advertised their favorite Democrat in 1888.

11. Dr. Howard Dean had many supporters in George W. Bush's home state in 2004.

12. Titche-Goettinger, a Dallas department store, showed its support for Roosevelt's National Relief Act during the 1930s.

13. A Roosevelt birthday party celebrated in Longview.

PLATE 25

Presidential Elections and Texas

1. Judson Harmon of Ohio contested Woodrow Wilson for the Texas vote in 1912.

2. Governor Dolph Briscoe did not support Republicans, but his friends supported Gerald Ford in 1976.

3. This election-night Carter button was worn by Azie Taylor Morton. Ms. Morton, from Dale, Texas, was the first African American to serve as treasurer of the United States.

4. In the 2004 race, Democratic candidate John Kerry had his supporters in George W. Bush's home state.

5. This lapel pin is on-target; Texas loved Ronald Reagan.

6. 1936 marked the Texas Centennial and the first re-election bid for the Roosevelt-Garner ticket. To celebrate the centennial, the Texas Young Democrats minted this coin. One side shows Roosevelt and Garner. The reverse side pictures the rear of an elephant. Heads, you win; tails, you lose.

7. Longhorns for Nixon in 1968.

8. Favorite son Senator Ralph Yarborough did not make a serious run for president in 1972. His supporters wished he would have.

9. Fort Worth oilman Eddie Childs was famous for his radio spots, when he told his fellow Texans what made him mad (usually Democrats). This button exhorts voters to "Make Eddie Glad" by voting for Reagan in 1980.

10. Similar to turn-of-the-century trade cards that supported candidates and merchandise or merchants, this button from an El Paso creamery supported Jimmy Carter.

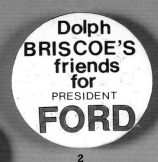

1

TEXAS HARMON DEMOCRATIC CLUB
HARMON-E

2

Dolph
BRISCOE'S
friends
for
PRESIDENT
FORD

8

72
YARBOROUGH
for PRESIDENT

3

CARTER
MONDALE
AZIE TAYLOR
MORTON
ELECTION
NIGHT
November 4, 1980

6

4

TEXAS for Kerry
Edwards '04

5

Texas
Reagan

9

MAKE EDDIE GLAD
VOTE
REAGAN
1980

10

I LIKE
CARTER and
SAN FRANCISCO
CREAMERY
EL PASO

7

NIXON AGNEW

1

3

3

3

2

4

PLATE 26

Presidential Elections and Texas

1. William Jennings Bryan had support in Grapevine, Texas, in 1896. The ribbon was found in my wife's grandmother's attic in Ennis.

2. Election-night button from Austin celebrating Clinton's 1996 victory.

3. A set of buttons made for Longhorns and Aggies during the 1972 election.

4. In 1948, Harry Truman was not as popular in Texas as he is now, although raising taxes has not increased in popularity.

PLATE 27

Presidential Elections and Texas

1. Dwight Eisenhower carried Texas in 1952 and 1956. Although raised in Kansas, Eisenhower is a native Texan, having been born in Denison.

2. Ronald Reagan's popularity in Texas survives his death. He carried Texas in 1980 and 1984.

3. While Reagan was popular, Walter Mondale supporters proudly wore these Texas buttons in 1984.

4. In 1960, Richard Nixon lost to John Kennedy. It was this ubiquitous button at Ridglea Hills Elementary in Fort Worth that fired my desire to wear my Kennedy-Johnson buttons given to me by my dad.

ANOTHER **TEXAN** FOR **IKE**

1

IKE

1

IKE

1

IKE TEXAS

1

I LIKE IKE

1

REAGAN COUNTRY

2

I'M FOR EISENHOWER AND NIXON

1

'84 '84

TEXANS FOR MONDALE

'84

3

NIXON

4

TEXAS *for* **GOLDWATER**

1

DEMOCRATS
Let's send
Ronnie and Phil
the same message we sent Bill
MOVING VAN

4

The Ticket for Tarrant County
Bill Clinton & Al Gore

2

TRAVIS COUNTY
Gore Lieberman
YOU'VE GOT THE POWER

5

TEXANS FOR FORD

6

TEXANS FOR MUSKIE '72

9

CARTER RE-ELECT 1980

3

LUBBOCK ♥'S
'92 **Clinton** GORE

PAID FOR LUBBOCK CO DEMO PARTY 1116 BROADWAY LUB TX 79401 TREASURER HARVEY MADISON

7

TEXANS FOR McCAIN
www.mccaintexas.com

8

PLATE 28

Presidential Elections and Texas

1. In 1964, Barry Goldwater's Texas supporters mounted a vigorous campaign in President Johnson's home state.

2. Tarrant County supporters of Al Gore and Bill Clinton wore this button in 1996.

3. Southerner Jimmy Carter failed to carry Texas in 1980.

4. In 1982, Democrat gubernatorial candidate Mark White defeated Republican incumbent Bill Clements. In 1984, the Democrats hoped to do the same to Ronald Reagan and Phil Gramm. They didn't succeed.

5. Travis County for Al Gore in 2000.

6. In 1976, Texas supporters of Gerald Ford put out this button.

7. In 1992, these Lubbock Democrats supported Bill Clinton over former fellow West Texan George H. W. Bush.

8. Arizona Republican Senator John McCain had a lot of supporters in Governor Bush's home state in 2000.

9. Edmund Muskie is celebrated in this Texas-made button.

PLATE 29

Kennedy and Johnson, 1960

 he Texan's Ticket" was the Kennedy-Johnson slogan in 1960. Johnson helped the Democrats carry the state. These posters are quite rare.

THE TEXAN'S TICKET

KENNEDY JOHNSON

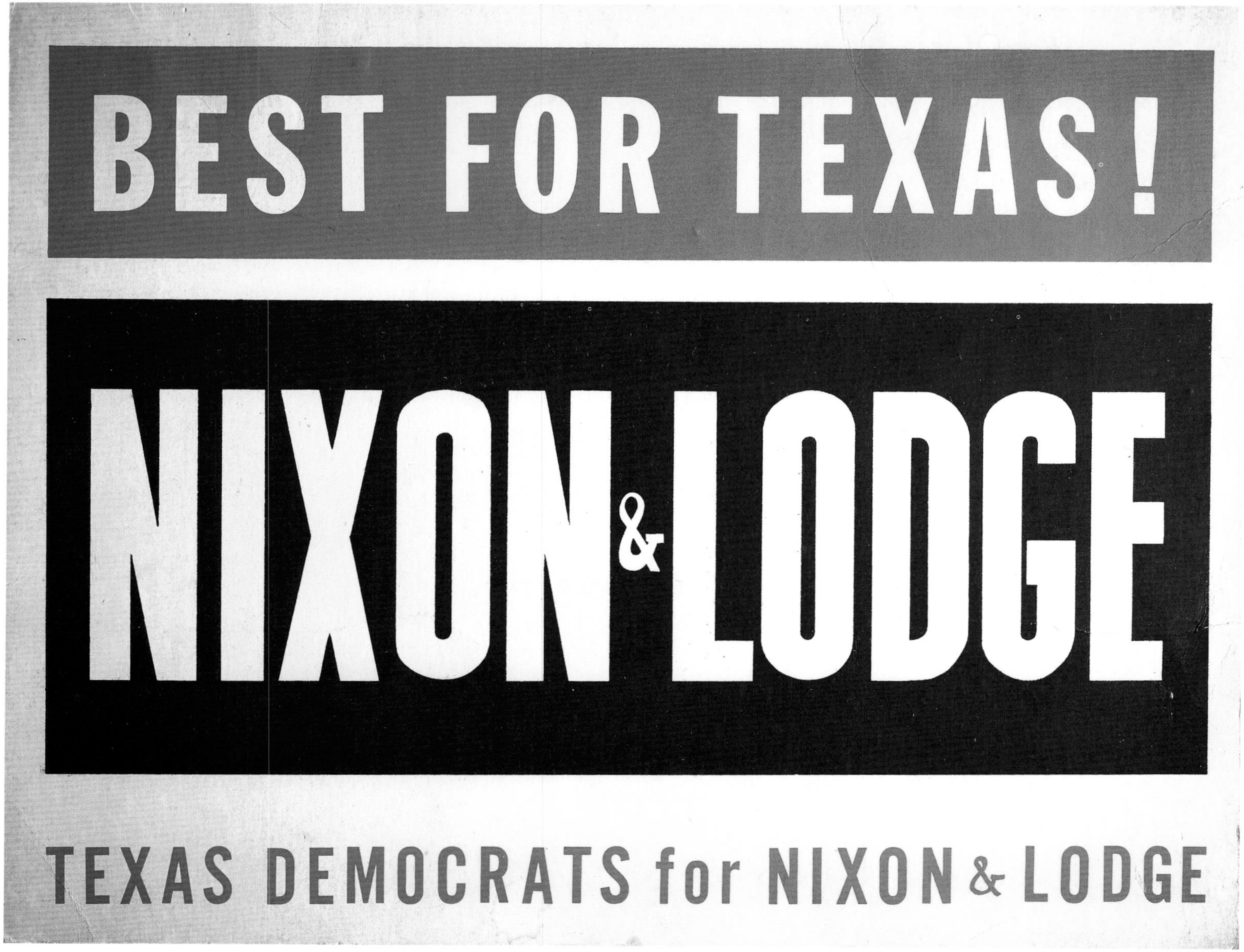
BEST FOR TEXAS!
NIXON & LODGE
TEXAS DEMOCRATS for NIXON & LODGE

PLATE 30

Nixon and Lodge, 1960

While some Texas Democrats were pushing for Kennedy-Johnson, other Texas Democrats supported the Nixon-Lodge ticket as "Best for Texas!"

PLATE 31

Ross Perot

Ross Perot, a Dallas computer magnate, ran an independent campaign for president in 1992. Forming his own party, Perot won close to twenty percent of the popular vote in the general election.

1. In the 1992 election, Connecticut-born Texas resident George H. W. Bush ran against Texas-born Perot, hence the slogan "The Real Texan" on this button.

2. A Styrofoam car antenna ball with a Perot slogan.

3. "Make Ross Boss": A blinking, battery-operated red light is located in the *o* in "Ross." Starting in the early 1980s, buttons flashed, blinked, and played music.

PEROT (the REAL TEXAN) FOR PRESIDENT

1

PEROT

PEROT

2

PEROT

TEXANS FOR ROSS PEROT '92

MAKE ROSS Boss

3

PEROT

TARRANT COUNTY PEROT VOLUNTEER

THE COUNTRY THE TIME THE MAN 1992

Arriba PEROT

I'M MAD AS HELL, AND I'M NOT GOING TO TAKE IT ANYMORE! PEROT INDEPENDENT for PRESIDENT '92

TEXANS for PEROT

Ross PEROT for PRESIDENT '92

Texas Conventions

In 1928, Democrats held Texas's first national political convention in Houston. Some items reminded voters of the Republican scandal known as Teapot Dome. Buttons, postcards, and even candy boxes showed the marriage of Texas longhorn and Democratic donkey.

In 1984, Dallas hosted the Republican convention, as did Houston in 1992 for favorite son George H. W. Bush.

Most items on page 65 are from the Jack Wilson Collection.

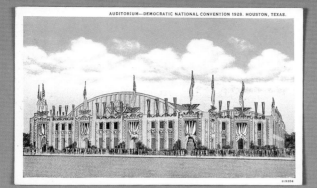

AUDITORIUM—DEMOCRATIC NATIONAL CONVENTION 1928. HOUSTON, TEXAS.

WHY I AM VOTING THE DEMOCRATIC TICKET

NAT. DEMOCRATIC CONVENTION, HOUSTON, TEX. JUNE 26-28

"ME-TOO"

NATIONAL DEMOCRATIC CONVENTION
HOUSTON 1928

AL. SMITH
FOR PRESIDENT

SOUVENIR OF
NATIONAL
DEMOCRATIC
CONVENTION

HOUSTON, TEXAS
JUNE, 1928

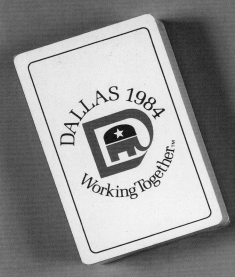

BUSH ★ QUAYLE

HOUSTON '92

TEXAS REPUBLICANS A MAJORITY ... FOR A CHANGE

The Official Airline Of The Republican National Convention

1992 REPUBLICAN NATIONAL CONVENTION

HOUSTON TEXAS

Continental

Welcome Republican National Convention

Houston Texas

August 17-20 1992

PRESIDENT GEORGE BUSH

REPUBLICAN NATIONAL CONVENTION AUGUST 17-20, 1992

HOUSTON, TEXAS

RNC 1992 HOUSTON HOLIDAY INN CROWNE PLAZA

RNC 1992 HOUSTON, TEXAS

Stand By Your Man!

REPUBLICAN CONVENTION

Bush '92 Quayle

HOUSTON ASTRODOME

Texas Governor

Candidates for Texas governor, winners and losers, have given the people of Texas a sparkling variety of political items. The usual buttons and bumper stickers have pictures, drawings, and slogans like "Me for Ma," "Another Man for Ann," and "A Lady for Claytie." Buttons designed like Texas Ranger badges; cattle ear-tags; and bumper stickers with Southwest Conference colors barely describe the available variety. Though the real political power in Texas lies in the legislature, many prominent Texans have striven to be governor. Knowing how to use the "bully pulpit" helps a strong personality become a strong governor.

PLATE 35

Texas Governor

1. Clayton Williams, Republican from Midland, lost in 1990 to Ann Richards.

2. Mark White, Democrat from Henderson, defeated Bill Clements in 1982. He lost to Clements in 1986.

3. Marty Akins, a Democrat, dropped out of the 2002 governor's race and ran a losing race for state comptroller against Carole Strayhorn.

4. Don Crowder, a Dallas-area lawyer, ran for the Democratic nomination in 1986. One of his cases, in which he successfully defended a hatchet-wielding housewife in a sensational murder trial, was turned into a made-for-TV movie.

5. Richard "Kinky" Friedman made a bid for governor in 2006 on the platform "How hard could it be?" The popular singer and author ran unsuccessfully for justice of the peace in Kerrville in the 1980s.

MARTY **AKINS** *for* **GOVERNOR**

2002

3

Clayton Williams

1

CROWDER FOR GOVERNOR

4

Mark White FOR GOVERNOR

2

Women For **Mark White** FOR GOVERNOR

2

KINKY FRIEDMAN **GOVERNOR 2006**

www.KinkyFriedman.com

5

Make Texas Great Again

Clayton Williams FOR GOVERNOR

1

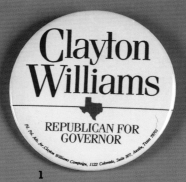

Clayton Williams

REPUBLICAN FOR GOVERNOR

1

A Lady for **CLAYTIE**

1

Clayton Williams FOR GOVERNOR

1

RE-ELECT MARK WHITE GOVERNOR

DEMOCRAT

2

KINKY FRIEDMAN
GOVERNOR 2006

GARRY MAURO
Governor

3

Democrat **Vote**
★ **Bill**
LYON
For
GOVERNOR

2

WorldPeace
Governor
2002

8

Adams   Governor
★★★★★★★★★★★★★★★★★★★★★★★
A Democrat For A New Republic of Texas

6

POWER 100

for MAURO
for GOVERNOR

3

MARK
WHITE
NIGHT
1981

1

TEXAS NEEDS CASH
VOTE
BUBBLES CASH
GOVERNOR - '90
DALLAS, TX

5

BRISCOE
for Texas

4

STUDENTS FOR
★ **TONY**
SANCHEZ
for Texas Governor
www.tonysanchez.com

7

WE ARE STICK'N WITH
TONY SANCHEZ

7

Sportsmen
for
Sanchez

POL. AD. PD. BY TONY SANCHEZ FOR GOVERNOR, INC. 6207 BEE CAVE RD, STE. 250 AUSTIN, TX 78746 JOE W. CRAWFORD TREAS.

7

PLATE 36

Texas Governor

1. The plastic keychain is from a White fund-raiser in 1981.

2. Bill Lyon was a long-shot candidate in 2002 from Waxahachie.

3. Garry Mauro, an Austin Democrat, lost to George W. Bush in 1998.

4. Andy Briscoe, a distant cousin of Dolph Briscoe, lost in the Democratic primary in 1986.

5. Bubbles Cash, a dancer from Dallas, did not do well in her 1990 race.

6. Stanley Adams, an indicted savings-and-loan official, ran for governor in 1986. Like Ms. Cash, he did not do well.

7. Despite spending millions of his own dollars, Laredo banker Tony Sanchez was defeated by incumbent Rick Perry in 2002.

8. Houston lawyer John WorldPeace was as successful as his name in 2002.

PLATE 37

Texas Governor

1. Tom Hunter, Democrat from Wichita Falls, ran unsuccessfully in 1932, 1934, 1936, and 1938.

2. O. B. Colquitt, Democrat from Terrell, won in 1910 and 1912.

3. Lynch Davidson, Democrat from Houston, lost in 1920 and 1924.

4. William McCraw, Democrat from Dallas, lost in 1938.

5. Jimmy Allred, Democrat from Wichita Falls (window sticker), won in 1934 and 1936.

6. W. F. Ramsey, Democrat from Dallas, lost in 1912.

7. Pat Neff, Democrat from Waco, won in 1922 and 1924.

8. Beauford Jester (emery board), Democrat from Corsicana, won in 1946 and 1948. Jester died in office and was replaced by Allan Shivers.

9. Charles Culberson, Democrat from Fort Worth–Dallas, won in 1894 and 1896. The button is from an old set of state governor buttons.

10. Republican Jack Culbertson lost in 1920.

11. Orville Bullington, Republican from Wichita Falls, lost in 1932.

12. William Poindexter, Democrat from Cleburne, lost in 1910.

FOR
**TOM
HUNTER**
GOVERNOR

1

FOR GOVERNOR
O. B. COLQUITT

2

FOR GOVERNOR
LYNCH DAVIDSON

3

"A Texan for Texas"
WILLIAM
McCRAW

184

FOR
GOVERNOR

4

1

For a Texas Recovery

TOM HUNTER
FOR
Governor

WHAT HOME FOLKS THINK

Results of the first primary in
Wichita Falls, home of both run-off
candidates, were:

Wichita County—
    Hunter—5,013
    Allred—3,762

Wichita Falls—
    Hunter—2,988
    Allred—2,112

Voting precinct in which both candidates reside:
    Hunter—101
    Allred—74

AN ADDRESS TO THE VOTERS

FOR GOVERNOR W. F. RAMSEY

6

PAT NEFF
FOR GOVERNOR

7

Follow THE PEOPLE'S PATH
WITH
BEAUFORD JESTER for GOVERNOR

8

CHARLES A. CULBERSON
GOV. TEXAS 1895-1899

9

FOR GOVERNOR

JACK CULBERTSON

10

5

ALLRED

1

ORVILLE
BULLINGTON
for
GOVERNOR

11

W. POINDEXTER
FOR GOVERNOR

12

R.V. DAVIDSON
Candidate for Governor

"BY HIS WORK YE SHALL KNOW HIM"

1

FOR GOVERNOR
R.V. DAVIDSON

1

CLINT C. SMALL
FOR GOVERNOR

2

ALL FOR BELL FOR ALL FOR BELL FOR

3

FOR GOVERNOR
C.K. BELL

5

ROSS STERLING FOR GOVERNOR

4

THOMPSON FOR GOVERNOR

7

TEXAS FOR SIMPSON

6

FOR GOVERNOR
JOHN N. SIMPSON

6

ERNEST THOMPSON

FOR GOVERNOR

VOTE FOR A MAN WITH
A SOUND RECORD
OF PUBLIC
SERVICE

7

Elect
HARRY HINES
GOVERNOR

TEXAS NEEDS HIM
A Doer—Not a Promiser

(Over)

8

STICK WITH—
STEVENSON
for GOVERNOR

9

PLATE 38

Texas Governor

1. Former Attorney General R. V. Davidson (postcard and button), Democrat from Galveston, lost in 1910.

2. Clint Small, Democrat from Amarillo, lost in 1934.

3. Tom Ball, Democrat from Houston, lost in 1914.

4. Ross Sterling, Democrat from Houston, won in 1930.

5. C. K. Bell, Democrat from Fort Worth, lost in 1906, the year that marked the state's first primary election.

6. John Simpson (watch fob and button), Republican from Dallas, lost in 1908.

7. Ernest O. Thompson (button and brochure), Democrat from Austin, lost in 1938.

8. Harry Hines (palm card), Democrat from Dallas, lost in 1940.

9. Coke Stevenson (window sticker), Democrat from Junction, won in 1942 and 1944.

PLATE 39

Texas Governor

1. Eugene Locke (button and brochure), Democrat from Dallas. Despite his ubiquitous radio jingle, "Eugene Locke Should Be Governor of Texas, The Governor of Texas Should Be Eugene Locke," he lost in 1968.

2. Don Yarborough, Democrat from Houston, led the Democratic primary but lost to Preston Smith in a 1968 runoff.

3. Bob Armstrong, Democrat from Austin, lost in the Democratic primary in 1982.

4. John Hill, Democrat from Houston, lost in the 1968 Democratic primary and in the 1978 general election. He served as secretary of state, attorney general, and chief justice of the Texas Supreme Court.

5. Ramsey Muñiz, La Raza Unida's candidate from Corpus Christi, lost in 1972 and 1974.

6. Paul Eggers, Republican from Wichita Falls, lost in 1970.

7. Oscar Holcombe, Democrat from Houston and former Houston mayor, lost in the 1950s.

8. Hank Grover (emery board and button), Republican from Houston, lost in 1972 and 1974.

9. Ben Barnes, Democrat from DeLeon, lost the 1972 primary largely due to the Sharpstown Stock-Fraud Scandal, which occurred during his term as lieutenant governor.

10. Jack Cox, Republican from Midland, lost to Price Daniel in the 1960 Democratic primary and to John Connally in the 1962 general election.

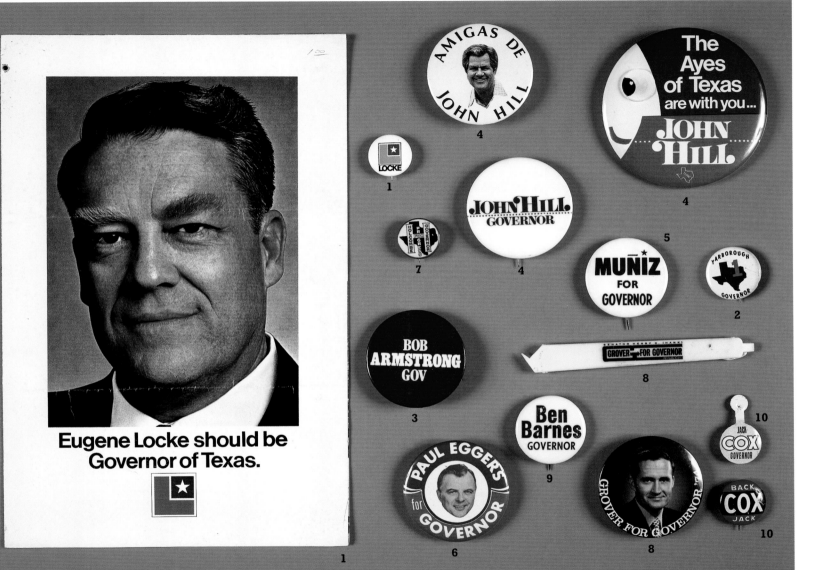

PLATE 40

Texas Governor

1. The bumper-sticker is probably from a Ralph Yarborough campaign, given that Yarborough and Shivers ran against each other twice.

2. "Platform of Edwin A. Walker," Democrat from Dallas. Lee Harvey Oswald supposedly shot through General Walker's front window prior to the Kennedy assassination. Walker lost in the Democratic primary in 1978.

3. Ray Hutchison, Republican from Dallas, married to U.S. Senator Kay Bailey Hutchison, lost in the Republican primary in 1978.

4. James Granberry, Republican from Lubbock, lost in 1974.

5. Allan Shivers (antenna flag and button), Democrat from Austin and Woodville, won in 1950, replacing the deceased Beauford Jester in 1952 as both the Democratic and Republican candidate and in 1954.

6. A cloth-covered Don Yarborough button from 1968.

PLATE 41

Texas Governor

1. Stereo card of Governor Joseph Sayers, Democrat from Bastrop, and President William McKinley at the Alamo. Sayers was elected in 1898 and 1900.

2. Postcard from 1905 of Governor Samuel W. T. Lanham, Democrat from Weatherford, elected in 1902 and 1904.

3. Tom Campbell (button and postcard), was elected governor of Texas in 1906 and 1908. As a Democrat and a lawyer from Palestine, he was allied with Governor Hogg.

4. John H. Reagan was running for governor in 1894 when this pamphlet was published. He did not win. He was a longtime force in Texas Democratic politics, serving as county judge in Henderson County, district judge, U.S. congressman, U.S. senator, and the first chairman of the Texas Railroad Commission. The "Old Roman" also served as postmaster general of the Confederacy.

On historic ground—President McKinley and Governor Sayers at Plaza Alamo, San Antonio, Texas. Copyright 1901 by Underwood. Underwood & Underwood, Publishers, New York, London, Toronto-Canada, Ottawa-Kansas.

1

THE OFFICIAL STATE SEAL AND GOVERNOR POST CARD

1905-1907

Hon. SAMUEL W. T. LANHAM,
Governor of the State of Texas

COPYRIGHTED 1905, U. S. POST CARD COMPANY
WILMINGTON, DEL.

2

Governor's Mansion and Governor Tom M. Campbell, Austin, Tex.

3

FOR GOVERNOR
TOM M. CAMPBELL

2

(SUPPLEMENT.)

ANNOUNCEMENT
OF
JOHN H. REAGAN
As a Candidate for Governor.

BRIEF OUTLINE OF HIS VIEWS ON PENDING ISSUES—STATE AND FEDERAL.

AUSTIN, TEXAS, May 23, 1894.

To the People of Texas:

In answer to solicitations too numerous and respectable to be disregarded, I announce myself a candidate for nomination for the office of Governor of Texas by the State Democratic Convention, which is to meet at Dallas in August.

In making this announcement, it is proper that I should indicate some of the measures and policies, State and Federal, which are necessary to the public welfare.

EXISTING LAWS.

I approve and will endeavor to have the following named laws faithfully executed:

1. The Railroad Commission Law of Texas as it now exists, subject to such changes only as may become necessary to its greater perfection.

2. The Alien Land Law, which prevents persons not citizens of the United States from holding title to land in this State for more than fifteen years.

3. The Municipal Bond Law, which prohibits the issuance of bonds by counties, towns and cities except for the purposes specified.

4. The Corporation Land Law, which prohibits the further operation of land corporations, and requires those now owning lands in this State to sell them within fifteen years.

5. The Railroad Stock and Bond Law, which prohibits the issuance of fictitious stock and bonds and other indebtedness by railway companies.

6. The law which reserves all our public domain for the use of actual settlers, in suitable quantities, at low price on long time.

7. And generally all the laws for the protection of life, liberty, and property.

PROPOSED MEASURES.

I will, if elected Governor, unless otherwise directed by the State Democratic Convention, advocate such laws and policy as will insure:

1. The economical administration of the Government in all its departments, preserving the efficiency of the public service.

2. The revision of the laws in relation to the fees and allowances to district attorneys, sheriffs, and clerks, and a modification of the laws relating to the service of attachments on witnesses in distant counties.

3. A considerable reduction of the expenditures of the State could be made, without injury to the public service, by a reorganization of the judicial districts, a reduction of their number, and an equalization of the duties of the judges.

4. Provisions for the transfer of fees over and above a reasonable compensation, to be fixed by law, to the several counties in which such officers respectively reside.

5. The reduction of the force and expense of the several departments and institutions to actual public necessity, consistent with the efficiency of the service.

6. Such laws as will render more perfect the policy of working the penal convicts on State account and prevent their competition with free labor.

7. Such legislation as will more perfectly protect laborers, material men, and mechanics against loss and injustice.

8. Such legislation as may be necessary to complete the work of suppressing

4

PLATE 42

W. Lee "Pappy" O'Daniel

O'Daniel, a flour salesman and radio announcer, ran for governor after being encouraged to do so by his radio audience. With his Hillbilly Boys and attractive family, he campaigned across the state and was elected governor in 1938 and 1940. In 1941, he defeated Lyndon Johnson for the U.S. Senate seat left vacant by the death of Morris Sheppard. He served until 1948. His unsuccessful comeback campaigns for governor in 1956 and 1958 showed his time had come and gone.

1. Palm cards with "Beautiful Texas" (see Plate 43), his self-penned theme song, on the reverse.

2. He used these flour barrels and sacks for campaign fund-raising.

W. LEE O'DANIEL

The "Common Citizen's" Candidate For
UNITED STATES SENATOR

2

W. LEE O'DANIEL

The "Common Citizen's" Candidate for

United States Senator

When elected United States Senator from Texas I shall continue to honestly and faithfully perform my Official duties with fairness to all and special favors to none.

W. Lee O'Daniel

(over)

1

W. LEE O'DANIEL

The "Common Citizen's" Candidate For

GOVERNOR

State Headquarters --- Fort Worth

If and when I am elected Governor of Texas I shall honestly and faithfully perform the duties of that office with fairness to all and special favors to none.

W. Lee O'Daniel

(over)

1

THE STATE OF TEXAS

1939

INAUGURAL RECEPTION
JANUARY SEVENTEENTH

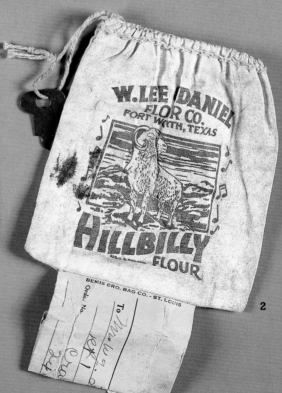

W. LEE O'DANIEL
FLOR CO.
FORT WORTH, TEXAS

HILLBILLY
FLOUR

BEMIS BRO. BAG CO. - ST. LOUIS

2

OFFICIAL SOUVENIR PROGRAM

inauguration of governor
W. lee o'daniel
austin, tex.   jan. 17, 1939

1

United States Senate Chamber

Washington, D.C. June 30 1947

Admit Mr. Ted Gardner

To the reserved gallery

For 80TH CONGRESS

W. Lee O'Daniel

U.S. SENATOR

2

"Beautiful Texas"
Composed by
W. LEE O'DANIEL

1
You have all read the beautiful stories
Of the countries far over the sea.
From whence came our ancestors
To establish this land of the free.
There are some folks who still like to travel
To see what they have over there.
But when they go look, it's not like the book,
And they find there is none to compare.

CHORUS
(Oh) Beautiful, beautiful Texas,
Where the beautiful bluebonnets grow.
We're proud of our forefathers
Who fought at the Alamo.
You can live on the plains or the mountain
Or down where the sea breezes blow.
And you're still in beautiful Texas,
The most beautiful State that we know.

2
You can travel on beautiful highways
By the city, the village, and farm.
Or sail up above on the skyways,
And the beauty below you will charm;
White cotton, green forests, blue rivers,
Golden wheat fields, and fruit trees that bear;
You can look till doomsday, and then you will say
That Texas has beauty to spare.

3
In this song about beautiful Texas,
There's one thing we just have to say
About six million people,
Who are proud they're here to stay.
It's great to be healthy and happy,
And that seems to be our good fate,
So let us all smile—for life is worth while
When we live in this beautiful State.

COPYRIGHTED MARCH 8, 1934

My Platform:
"The Ten Commandments"

My Motto:
"The Golden Rule"

My Slogan:
"Preserve Democracy"

(over)

LIGHT CRUST FLOUR
HAPPY DAYS ARE HERE AGAIN

3

LIGHT CRUST FLOUR
HAPPY DAYS ARE HERE AGAIN
FT. WORTH

3

LIGHT CRUST DOUGHBOYS
MEMBER "SAVE YOUR OWN LIFE CLUB"

3

PLATE 43

W. Lee "Pappy" O'Daniel

1. This button with ribbons is from O'Daniel's first inauguration. Breaking with tradition, he held the inauguration in Texas Memorial Stadium.

2. Senators give these Senate Chamber passes to constituents.

3. The "Light Crust Flour" buttons are both advertising and campaign-related items.

PLATE 44

llan Shivers was elected governor in 1952 and 1954.

FOR TEXAS AND SHIVERS

320

DEMOCRAT

Connally

GOVERNOR

PLATE 45

John Connally, from Floresville, cut his political teeth as an assistant to Lyndon Johnson. Originally a Democrat, he served as President Kennedy's secretary of the Navy. He was elected governor in 1962, 1964, and 1966. He was wounded while riding in President Kennedy's motorcade in Dallas on November 22, 1963. After leaving the governor's office, he practiced law, and then he served as secretary of the treasury under President Nixon.

In 1973, after LBJ's death, he switched his affiliation to the Republican Party. He ran as a Republican in the 1980 presidential election, triggering the 1979 quorum-busting Killer Bees incident in the Texas Senate. His race was unsuccessful, and he retired from elective politics after the campaign.

1. This John Connally poster came out of the Fort Worth Democratic headquarters in 1964. Connally had been living in Fort Worth when he first ran for governor.

PLATE 46

umper stickers printed in Southwest Conference colors were the idea of Julian and Annis Read, who ran all of Connally's campaigns.

'62 BAYLOR **Connally** GOVERNOR

'62 TECH **Connally** GOVERNOR

'62 RICE **Connally** GOVERNOR

'62 TCU **Connally** GOVERNOR

'62 SMU **Connally** GOVERNOR

'62 TEXAS **Connally** GOVERNOR

'62 A & M **Connally** GOVERNOR

GOVERNOR AND MRS. CLEMENTS ★ AUSTIN TEXAS ★ JANUARY 16, 1979
INAUGURATION

1

CLEMENTS
G★VERN★R

Pol. adv. paid by
Governor Clements Comm.
Tom B. Rhodes, Treas.
807 Brazos, Austin, Tx.

I Love The Guvenah!

GARLAND LOVES BILL CLEMENTS

2

INAUGURATION JANUARY 16, 1979
GOVERNOR BILL CLEMENTS

Bill Clements FOR GOVERNOR

Re-elect
CLEMENTS
G★VERN★R

Political advertisement paid by the Governor Clements Committee, 807 Brazos, Austin, Texas, 78701.

DEMOCRATS for CLEMENTS

RE-ELECT CLEMENTS GOVERNOR

CLEMENTS

PLATE 47

Bill Clements

Dallasite Bill Clements was the first Republican elected governor since Reconstruction. He won in 1978, lost in 1982, and was re-elected in 1986. A Texas history fan, he convinced James Michener to write *Texas* during the Texas sesquicentennial.

1. Button from the 1979 inauguration. Rita Clements, who later served on the U.T. Board of Regents, is also pictured.

2. The "Garland Loves Bill Clements" pin was made by former Garland mayor Charles Matthews, who was later elected to the Texas Railroad Commission.

PLATE 48

Ann Richards

nn Richards was a long-term political activist when she was elected Travis County commissioner in 1976. In 1982, she was elected Texas state treasurer, and in 1990 she became the second woman to be elected governor of Texas. She was defeated for re-election in 1994 by George W. Bush. Her political memorabilia is colorful, eclectic, and abundant.

1. No trademark hairdo yet in this 1978 county commissioner button.

2. A political postcard shows the governor holding her grandchild Lily at the 1988 Democratic National Convention.

3. An Austin leadership group honored the new governor with a breakfast and this large button on inauguration day.

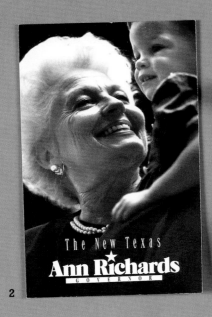

The New Texas
Ann Richards
GOVERNOR

2

1

Viva!
ANN
GOVERNOR

42

Ann Richards
for
STATE TREASURER

★ **Ann Richards**
GOVERNOR

LEADERSHIP TEXAS SALUTES
GOVERNOR ANN RICHARDS

3

INAUGURATION

JANUARY 15 1991

RE-ELECT MS. GOV.

Another Man
94
for
Governor Ann

GOVERNOR 1994

1

2

FOLD UP HERE ON SCORED LINE

FOLD DOWN HERE ON SCORED LINE

Ann Richards

For

State Treasurer

For An Honest Competent State Treasurer

Pd. Pol. Adv. Ann Richards State Treas. Comm. 3204 Nueces, Austin, Tx. 78705 John Wooley, Treas.

4

ABCDEFGHIJKLMNOPQRSTUVWXYZ

Aa

"READ EVERY DAY!!"

Ann W. Richards
GOVERNOR OF TEXAS

1   2   3   4   5   6   7

3

RICHARDS 1990

PLATE 49

Ann Richards

1. The cover of *Texas Monthly* magazine featured a picture of Governor Richards in white leather sitting on a white Harley. This button commemorates that popular picture.

2. This hard rubber figurine stood atop the inaugural cake in January, 1991.

3. This plastic ruler was given to schoolchildren who visited the governor's office. Richards is an avid supporter of reading.

4. A fold-up paper sun visor from the state treasurer's race.

PLATE 50

Rick Perry

Governor Rick Perry served as state representative, agriculture commissioner, and lieutenant governor prior to assuming the governorship upon George W. Bush's election as president. He was elected governor on his own in 2002.

1. In Texas, the campaigns for governor and lieutenant governor are separate, and in some races the candidates represent different parties. Rarely do candidates' names appear in tandem, as on this bumper sticker for Bush/Perry.

2. Rick Perry's brand is shown on these lapel pieces.

Bush ★ Perry

VOTE NOV. 3 FOR TEXAS

Paid for by Bill Thompson Advertising Specialties: P.O. Box 180453; Austin Tx 78718 (512) 244-9703

1

2

Rick **Perry**

FOR LIEUTENANT GOVERNOR

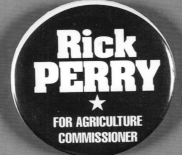

Rick **PERRY**
★
FOR AGRICULTURE
COMMISSIONER

2

Rick **Perry**

Political Advertisement paid for by Texans for Rick Perry

Rick Perry ★

FOR AGRICULTURE COMMISSIONER

Paid for by Texans for Rick Perry, William A. McKenzie, Treasurer.

TEXANOS POR
PERRY
GOBERNADOR

2003 GUBERNATORIAL INAUGURATION AUSTIN, TEXAS
Gov. Rick Perry
January 21, 2003

★ **PERRY**
GOVERNOR

MY REPUBLICAN DREAM TEAM
David Dewhurst for Lt. Gov.
Gov. Rick Perry
Greg Abbott for AG
John Cornyn for US Senate
THE DEMOCRAT'S NIGHTMARE

1

WBDT
Harvey Kronberg
VIP
INAUGURAL PARADE

Saluting   Saluting
Governor   Lt. Governor
Rick   David
Perry   Dewhurst

ANOTHER PROUD TEXAS AGGIE SUPPORTING...
BUSHPERRY
THE CONSERVATIVE TEAM FOR TEXAS IN '98
Political Advertisement paid for by Texans for Rick Perry, P.O. Box 2103, #217 Austin, TX 78768

3

★ **PERRY**
GOVERNOR

2

PLATE 51

Rick Perry

1. Again, the offices and campaigns are separate for governor, lieutenant governor, attorney general, and the U.S. Senate. In this button, however, the candidates constitute a "Republican Dream Team."

2. At each Texas governor's inaugural parade on Congress Avenue, the Wholesale Beer Distributors of Texas have a private reviewing stand. Invited guests are given a personalized button and ribbons. Harvey Kronberg, an Austin journalist, edits a popular political newsletter.

3. A proud graduate of Texas A&M, Governor Perry never fails to emphasize this close relationship to his alma mater.

PLATE 52

Lieutenant Governor

Candidates for lieutenant governor run for the popular vote statewide, separate from the gubernatorial candidate. The person holding this office is, in some minds, the most powerful politician in Texas. The Texas Constitution, written after Reconstruction, assigned little power to the governor's office. The Legislature is generally the most powerful of the three branches of government, and as presiding officer of the Senate, the lieutenant governor has a lot to say as to what becomes law and how taxes are spent. He (Texas has never had a female lieutenant governor) also appoints chairs and members to senate committees and serves as chair of the Legislative Budget Board, which has much to say about state spending. The lieutenant governor replaces the governor upon any vacancy in that office. This unique office encompasses both the executive and legislative branches of government.

1. Ben Ramsey, a Democrat from San Augustine, served as lieutenant governor for most of the 1950s. A loyal Democrat, he served as state party chair in 1955 and was twice elected to the Railroad Commission.

2. Manufactured by former Speaker Gib Lewis, these plastic devices with the lieutenant governor's seal can be attached to a plate and used to hold a piece of stemware. At the innumerable receptions a lieutenant governor must attend, it makes holding one's refreshments much easier.

3. A great button for a Texan. Republican Dallasite and former Nixon speechwriter Tex Lezar ran unsuccessfully against Bob Bullock in 1994.

4. Longtime East Texas politician Ralph Hall passed out these lucky pennies with the motto, "All for Hall from Rockwall."

5. "Byron Who? for Lt. Gov.," was Republican Byron Fullerton's campaign slogan in 1970. Fullerton, a law professor, became an artist in later years.

6. "Calculating" Coke Stevenson was elected lieutenant governor in 1938 and again in 1940. When Governor O'Daniel won a U.S. Senate seat in the 1941 special election, Stevenson became governor. In 1948, he was defeated for the U.S. Senate by Lyndon Johnson in the famous "landslide" election.

7. The newest lieutenant governor, David Dewhurst, is a rancher and loves to rope, thus his lapel pin, "Dewhurst Team Roper."

8. Ben Barnes, Democrat from DeLeon, was elected lieutenant governor in 1968 and 1970. At thirty, he was the youngest lieutenant governor ever. Earlier, he had served as the youngest Speaker of the House. His 1972 run for governor was undoubtedly derailed by the Sharpstown Stock Scandal.

9. In this satirical political cartoon, Ben Barnes is shown holding up Governor Preston Smith by the ears, a parody of the famous Lyndon Johnson photo that shows Johnson holding his beagle by the ears.

BEN RAMSEY
of San Augustine
for LIEUTENANT GOVERNOR
The Man Texans
Know and Respect

1

A MAN
TEXANS
KNOW
AND
RESPECT

Win with
BEN
RAMSEY
of
SAN AUGUSTINE
for
LIEUTENANT GOVERNOR

1

COKE
STEVENSON
of Kimble County
FOR
Lieutenant-Governor
Twice Speaker of the House
of Representatives
Presided over the House four years
without an appeal from his
decisions
8
"ECONOMY, EXPERIENCE, EFFICIENCY
IN GOVERNMENT"
(OVER)

6

9

LIEUTENANT GOVERNOR
THE STATE OF TEXAS

2

Tex!
for
Lt. Governor

3

RALPH M. HALL
FOR LT. GOVERNOR

4

7

BYRON
WHO?
FOR LT. GOV.

5

BARNES
FOR
LT. GOVERNOR

IDEAS ACTION ›
FULLERTON
LIEUTENANT GOVERNOR

BB
FOR TEXAS

1

8

Andy Andujar for State Senate
1

Betty Andujar State Senate
1

I WAS SERVED
SENATE DEMO. BBQ 1994
8

Armbrister
TEXAS SENATE
Paid for by Ken Armbrister for Senate Campaign, P.O. Box 5017, Victoria, Tx 77903.
9

JESSE
14

MONTFORD
11

A senator you can be proud of
BILL RATLIFF
STATE ★ SENATE
Paid for by Bill Ratliff for State Senate Campaign, Joe Sandlin, Treasurer.
3

STATE SENATOR
JOE J. BERNAL
13

MONCRIEF STATE SENATOR
2

RAY WATSON for STATE SENATE
4

SENATOR EDDIE LUCIO GOLF CLASSIC
10

JIMMY PHILLIPS for Performance not Promises

reelect JIMMY PHILLIPS your
FULL TIME PERSONAL SENATOR
Experienced—Courteous—Understanding—Friendly
12

MADE IN U.S.A.

MAYBE THEY MEANT 2 DAYS EVERY 140 YEARS "THE 69th"
5

SENATOR JEFF WENTWORTH
6

7

PLATE 53

Texas Senate

The Texas Senate has thirty-one members and is presided over by the lieutenant governor. With fewer members than the House, the Senate has a more relaxed feel, and difficult issues are often quietly worked out before ever reaching the floor for debate. That is not to say that debate cannot become rancorous at times, and in the Senate, a filibuster can shut down debate until the filibustering senator gives up. The Senate chamber is decorated with giant paintings of the battles of the Alamo and San Jacinto. With the image of Stephen F. Austin peering from behind the podium, Texas history is never far away.

1. Senator Betty Andujar and her husband, Dr. Andy Andujar, used identical buttons. Senator Andujar was the first woman to be a member of the Texas Senate, and the first Republican state senator since Reconstruction. When the senator passed away, her husband made an unsuccessful attempt to replace her.

2. Mike Moncrief, from Fort Worth, was elected to the Senate after serving as Tarrant County judge. He was elected mayor of Fort Worth in 2003.

3. Bill Ratliff, from Mount Pleasant, was elected lieutenant governor by the Senate in December of 2000. He replaced Rick Perry, who had become governor upon George W. Bush's election as president.

4. A Murray Watson thimble. Watson served as Waco's senator beginning in 1967.

5. This button, issued during the 69th Legislature (1985–1986), suggests that the Texas Constitution should have required legislative sessions lasting 2 days every 140 years instead of 140 days every 2 years. Some might agree.

6. Republican Jeff Wentworth, from San Antonio, can shed light on any issue with this political flashlight.

7. Senator Oscar Mauzy of Dallas, one of the "Killer Bees," handed out these bee pins at a party celebrating the success of the quorum-busting group of senators.

8. The Senate Democratic Caucus held a fund-raising barbeque in 1993 and handed out this button.

9. Senator Ken Armbrister, Democrat from Victoria, has carried some of the most important water legislation in recent years and is an expert on Senate traditions.

10. Eddie Lucio has an annual golf tournament/fund-raiser. Hats, tees, and other golf/political memorabilia are handed out during the tournament.

11. John Montford, a Lubbock Democrat, has served Texas as a criminal district attorney, state senator, and chancellor of Texas Tech.

12. Senator Jimmy Phillips of Brazoria County used matches, pencils, and this paper gun that, when snapped, makes a popping sound.

13. There are few Texas tabs around, but San Antonio Senator Joe Bernal produced one of the best examples.

14. Jesse George of Lubbock lost this Senate race, but scored a win with this windmill lapel pin.

PLATE 54

Texas Senate

1. Lubbock senator Doc Blanchard passed out these pink and black mirrors at his Governor for a Day celebration. During each session and interim, the Senate president is selected to serve in the absence of the lieutenant governor. On a given day when both the governor and lieutenant governor are out of state, the Senate president pro tem becomes governor for a day, and a celebration is held at the Capitol.

2. Laredo senator Judith Zaffirini has some of the most attractive memorabilia, such as buttons and mugs.

3. Ray Farabee, from Wichita Falls, served in the Senate from 1975 until 1986 when he became general counsel for the University of Texas system. His wife, Helen Farabee, ran for his vacant seat but died shortly before the election.

4. Eddie Bernice Johnson served in the Senate before being elected to Congress.

5. Ike Harris of Dallas was among the first Republicans to serve in the Texas Senate since Reconstruction and was the first Republican president pro tempore.

6. Senator Buster Brown, from Brazoria County, was first elected in 1980. He ran unsuccessfully for attorney general in 1990.

7. Don Hand, from San Antonio, served one term in the House and lost the election in which this rebus button was used.

8. Another pair of family buttons: Bill Moore, the Bull of the Brazos, served from 1949 until 1980. His daughter-in-law, Mary Moore, lost her race in 1998.

9. Carl Parker of Port Arthur was a master at senate debate.

SENATOR EDDIE BERNICE JOHNSON
OPENING THE DOORS TO THE FUTURE

4

H. J. (DOC)
BLANCHARD
Governor For A Day
August 15,
1969

1

GOVERNOR RAY FARABEE

MAY 4, 1985

3

Parker
for State Senate

Parker
for State Senate

Parker
for State Senate

Parker
for State Senate

Parker
for State Senate

Parker
for State Senate

Parker
for State Senate

Parker
for State Senate

Parker
for State Senate

Parker
for State Senate

Parker
for State Senate

Parker
for State Senate

Parker
for State Senate

Parker
for State Senate

9

I'M
FOR MOORE

8

Mary
MOORE
for Texas Senate

PD POL ADV BY MARY MOORE CAMPAIGN

8

ELECT
DON
HAND
STATE
SENATOR

7

IKE
STATE
SENATE

5

KEEP
SENATOR
BUSTER
BROWN

6

HELEN
FARABEE
makes us proud.

3

Judith
ZAFFIRINI
For Texas Senator

2

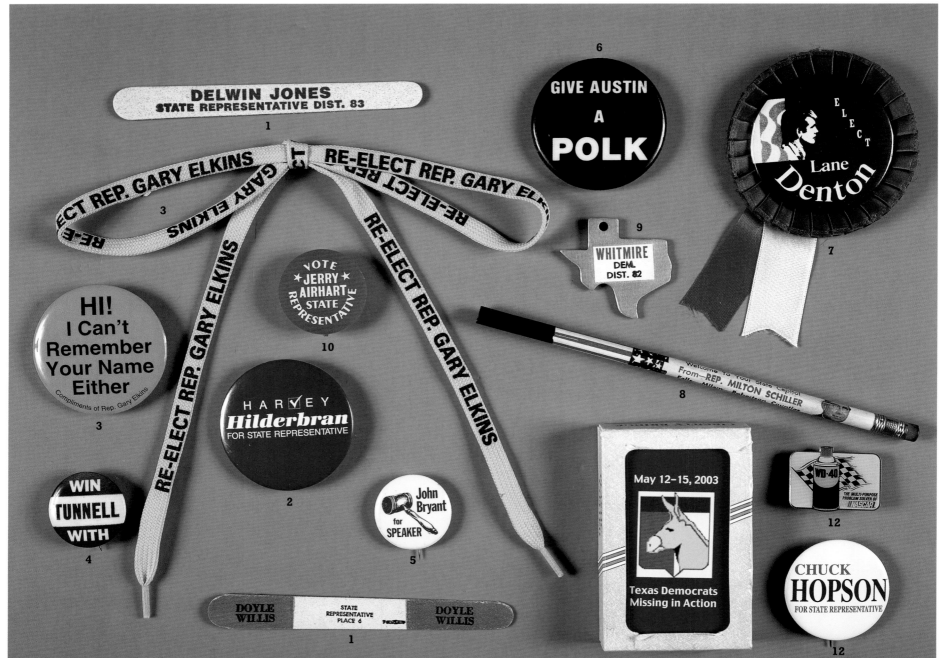

PLATE 55

Texas House of Representatives

The Texas House of Representatives is made up of 150 members and is presided over by a Speaker elected by the members. Unlike the clubby Senate, the House is often loud and frenetic. The types of political memorabilia are as varied as the personalities of the House members.

1. Delwin Jones, a Lubbock representative, has handed out emery boards for his races for the Texas House, Texas Senate, U.S. Congress, and tax assessor/collector. Doyle Willis also used them in his campaigns.

2. Harvey Hilderbran of Kerrville was the youngest House member at that time when first elected in 1987.

3. Republican Gary Elkins shows his sense of humor in his election material. As a freshman in 1995, he wore the button admitting he could not remember everyone either. Elkins used the only actual campaign shoestring I've seen, but many campaigns are run on one.

4. & 5. Byron Tunnell served as Speaker. John Bryant of Dallas did not.

6. Mary Polk won her seat from El Paso in 1978.

7. Lane Denton won his seat from Waco.

8. Milton Schiller, from Milam County, used pencils and thimbles in his rural district in the early 1960s.

9. Harris County Democrat John Whitmire made these die-cut Texas key rings in his father's garage in 1972.

10. From Lubbock County, Jerry Airhart used plastic bottle caps in a 1976 campaign.

11. In 2003, to destroy a quorum in a redistricting fight, House Democrats left the state for Ardmore, Oklahoma. This deck of cards contains pictures of all of the participants.

12. One of the Ardmore Democrats was Jacksonville Representative Chuck Hopson. He and a group of other representatives were called the WD-40s—white Democrats over forty.

13. Doyle Willis, a Democrat from Fort Worth, served in both the state Senate and House of Representatives.

PLATE 56

Texas House of Representatives

1. Mrs. L. G. Phares from Austin ran for the state House in the 1930s. She was the widow of Colonel L. G. Phares, the first director at the Texas Department of Public Safety.

2. George Moffett, from Chillicothe, represented a wide swath of West Texas in both the Texas House and Senate.

3. David Swinford used the ever-popular wooden nickel to campaign from Pampa.

4. Stan Schlueter, from the Killeen area, was a powerful chair of Ways and Means. During tax sessions, when tax bills were proposed, he was known to get a little testy. This button was issued in the mid 1980s—but no one believed it.

5. The Duke of Paducah in Cottle County, W. S. Bill Heatly was a strong voice for West Texas.

6. In the late 1960s or early 1970s, Bexar County Republicans put a team of candidates together. Ike Kampmann, Hans Helland, Henry Catto, and Walter McAlister lost, but won with the button design.

7. Buddy Ruiz lost in Austin.

8. Jim Rudd was a Democratic member from Brownfield. In 1991, he lost a Speaker's race to Pete Laney.

9. This Marvin Simpson, Jr., (Fort Worth), palm card is a good example of political advertising in the 1930s and 1940s.

10. W. A. Poage served in the Texas House in 1917 and 1919 from McClennan County. His son, W. R. Poage, from Waco, served in the U.S. Congress for many years.

11. Paul Floyd, from Harris County, used a golf ball marker in his race for the House.

12. Debra Danburg, from Houston, served several terms, beginning in 1981.

13. This San Antonio trigate button is rare in Texas. Along with Sylvia Mendelsohn's picture are those of Senator Frank Madla and Representative Ciro Rodriguez. Ms. Mendelsohn lost the runoff.

14. Ron Bird, from San Antonio, was elected to fly up to the Legislature in 1973.

3

DAVID
SWINFORD
STATE
REPRESENTATIVE
DISTRICT 87
512-463-0479

8

RUDD'S
RAIDERS

9

YOUR VOTE AND INFLUENCE SOLICITED

MARVIN B.
SIMPSON, JR.
FOR
REPRESENTATIVE
TARRANT COUNTY
PLACE 4
FIRST TIME TO SEEK PUBLIC OFFICE
20

FOR REPRESENTATIVE 114TH LEGISLATIVE DISTRICT

COMPOSED OF HARDEMAN, FOARD, KNOX, AND
KING COUNTIES

VOTE FOR
GEORGE MOFFETT

"The white haired West Texan who fought the big cities to a
standstill in the last Legislature and preserved the
rights of the small towns and country districts."

(SECOND TERM)

SUBJECT TO DEMOCRATIC PRIMARY JULY 23RD.

2

4

A KINDER
AND GENTLER
SCHLUETER

10

W.A. POAGE

11

PUTT FOR
PAUL FLOYD
State REP.
Harris County

5

6

LET'S CLEAN UP THE MESS IN AUSTIN

KAMPMANN
HELLAND
OREM
CATTO
McALISTER
VOTE REPUBLICAN

1

13

WE ALL SUPPORT

Sylvia Ruiz Mendelsohn
For State Rep. 118
Run off Election
Sat. June 21,1997

7

BUDDY RUIZ

STATE REPRESENTATIVE

14

RE-
ELECT
RON
BIRD
STATE
REPRESENTATIVE

12

DANBURG

14

ELECT
BIRD STATE REP.

Vote for

BILL CLAYTON

for State Representative

1

YOUR VOTE AND INFLUENCE
For
BILL CLAYTON
DEMOCRATIC NOMINEE
For
STATE REPRESENTATIVE
91st District
Is Greatly Appreciated and Denotes YOUR
Concern For Better Government
(OVER)

1

Your Vote & Influence
For
BILL CLAYTON
Democratic Candidate
**STATE
REPRESENTATIVE**
IS
GREATLY APPRECIATED

1

BILL
CLAYTON

1

I'm For
BILL CLAYTON
For
Better Government

1

I do hereby pledge my support to Bill Clayton

for Speaker of the 65th Legislative Session.

_____
Signature

_____
Date

2

Pete Laney

**Hometown Values
Real Leadership
Working For Us**

3

AMARILLO
WANTS A
RE-PETE

3

PLAINVIEW

for Pete's sake!

3

PLATE 57

West Texas House of Representatives Speakers

From 1975 to the present, West Texans have held the Speakership in the Texas House of Representatives. Until World War I, most Speakers were from East Texas, with a few from Central Texas. The trend changed around 1915, when hometowns such as Rotan, Amarillo, and Junction began to show up at the podium. Waggoner Carr (Lubbock) took over from 1957–1965. Since the election of Bill Clayton (Springlake) in 1975, followed by Gib Lewis (Fort Worth, "where the West begins"), Pete Laney (Hale Center), and Tom Craddick (Midland), West Texans have presided over the House.

1. A Bill Clayton thimble, matches, button, and palm card.

2. This card is what is commonly called a "pledge card." When Speaker candidates have seventy-six of these signed, they supposedly will be elected Speaker. Over the years, however, members have been known to sign more than one candidate's card. Speaker Clayton tells the story of a West Texas member who offered to mediate between three candidates because he had committed to all three.

3. Buttons from a Laney fund-raiser in Plainview.

PLATE 58

West Texas House of Representatives Speakers

1. Gib Lewis had gold lapel buttons made for his supporters.

2. A Gib Lewis key ring.

3. Tom Craddick brochure and bumper sticker from an early Midland campaign.

GIB LEWIS DAY
JANUARY 11, 1983

GIB

I'M A
"GIB"
LEWIS
GOOD GUY
STATE REP. PLACE 4
FOR

1

I LOVE
GIB

SPEAKER
Gil Lewis

2

RE-ELECT
TOM
CRADDICK

State Representative
76th District

3

CRADDICK

POL. ADV. PAID FOR BY RE-ELECT CRADDICK COMMITTEE, KATIE HECK, CHMN, 2603 HODGES, MIDLAND, TEX. 79705

STATE REPRESENTATIVE

3

RE-ELECT
CRADDICK
STATE REPRESENTATIVE

PLATE 59

Tom Craddick

om Craddick poster. Craddick served as the first Republican Speaker since Reconstruction.

PLATE 60

Attorney General

The attorney general is the state's lawyer in all civil matters. Despite the slant of some political advertisements, the attorney general does not represent the state in criminal matters. The Texas Constitution leaves that to the local district attorneys. The A.G. does, however, represent the state in matters ranging from oil and gas leases and revenues to tax issues. This office collects delinquent child support and works with local district attorneys on capital murder appeals. The position has sometimes been a stepping-stone to higher office. It propelled Price Daniel, Mark White, and Jimmy Allred to the governor's office and John Cornyn to the U.S. Senate.

1. Illustrating a successful grassroots campaign, these Jim Mattox buttons show how much a contributor has given. Mattox was a Democrat from Dallas who was elected A.G. in 1982 and 1986.

2. Democrat Mark White became attorney general in 1978 and moved into the governor's office in 1982. A portrait of an attractive family always makes good political sense.

3. Gerald Mann was elected attorney general in 1936 and 1938. Known as the "Little Red Arrow" from his All-American SMU football days, he ran unsuccessfully for the U.S. Senate in the 1941 special election.

4. Beginning in 1971, Max Sherman (Amarillo) served in the Texas Senate until 1977, when he accepted the job as president of West Texas State University in Canyon. In 1982, he ran unsuccessfully in the Democratic primary for A.G. His students at West Texas supported him with this button. He later served as dean of the LBJ school.

5. Dan Morales was first elected attorney general in 1990. Re-elected in 1994, he left office in 1998. After an ill-fated run for governor in 2002, Morales ended up with legal problems that brought his promising career to an end.

6. A palm card for Robert Calvert's unsuccessful 1938 run for attorney general. Calvert later served eleven years as the chief justice of the Texas Supreme Court. Interestingly, his card notes that he was raised in the State Orphanage Home in Corsicana.

7. Crawford Martin served as attorney general from 1966 to 1972. Like Bob Bullock and Robert Calvert, he was from Hillsboro. Martin also served as secretary of state.

8. Jim Baker of Houston ran for attorney general in 1978, losing to Mark White. He served as President Ford's undersecretary of commerce and was appointed secretary of the treasury by President Reagan and secretary of state by the first President Bush.

MATTOX
10

MATTOX
25

MATTOX
75

MATTOX
100

1

Mark White
FOR ATTORNEY GENERAL OF TEXAS.

2

Your Next
Attorney General

"I'd rather be a one-termer than a two-timer"

GERALD C. MANN

CANDIDATE FOR

ATTORNEY GENERAL

OF TEXAS

"Mann's The Man!"

9

3

MANN'S
THE
MAN

3

WT
BAX
MAX

Pd. Pol. Ad. E. T. Manning, Box 31625, Ama

4

**DAN
MORALES**
TEXAS ATTORNEY GENERAL

5

—VOTE FOR—
ROBERT W. CALVERT
OF HILL COUNTY, FOR
ATTORNEY GENERAL

Earnest—Honest—Fearless—Able

| Reared an over-alled boy in the State Orphans' Home at Corsi-cana, Texas. | Now Speaker of the House of Representatives and candidate for ATTORNEY GENERAL. |

Energetic—Ambitious—Reliable

184·   ·6·

AGE 13   AGE 33

"FROM STATE HOME TO STATE HOUSE"

6

**CRAWFORD
MARTIN**

7

**B
JIM
BAKER**
FOR ATTORNEY GENERAL

8

"As the state's chief legal officer, your next Attorney General should be independent of the political power structure that has dominated Texas government for too long."

Jim Baker

8

I will appreciate your vote for Beauford Jester of Navarro County for Railroad Commissioner in the run-off.

He has a constructive program to help win the war, for the production of oil and the regulation of transportation in Texas is vitally important in war time.

I know Beauford Jester to be a man of honesty and integrity. He is best qualified to fill this important office.

Beauford Jester
of Navarro County
CANDIDATE FOR
RAILROAD
COMMISSIONER
Second Primary
August 22, 1942

1

9

LAND
BOB
ARMSTRONG
COMMISSIONER

8

ELECT
DAN
KUBIAK
LAND COMMISSIONER

11

I TALK
with
Garry Mauro
TRASH

Charles
MATTHEWS
Railroad
Commissioner

2

★
MICHAEL
WILLIAMS
RAILROAD
COMMISSIONER

4

GUERRERO
TEAM 100

6

For Commissioner General Land Office
BASCOM GILES
OF TRAVIS COUNTY

Born on a farm near Manor, September, 1900

Knows the Land Office through 17 years experience under J. H. Walker, former Commissioner

Chief Abstracter State-Wide Tax Survey for past year and a half. Knows Texas Lands and Titles

Restore Confidence in the Administration of the Land Office

3 Subject to action Democratic Primary 1938
(Over)

10

John
Sharp
Texas
Democrat
for Railroad
Commissioner

5

Compliments
of
OLIN CULBERSON
Candidate
for
RAILROAD COMMISSIONER
Second Term

INSTANTLY ARRESTS HOSIERY RUNS

3

URIBE
for
Railroad
Commission

7

For COMMISSIONER
GENERAL LAND OFFICE
J. H. WALKER
PRESENT INCUMBENT; ASKING FOR
RE-ELECTION

He invites you to use the same care in selecting a commissioner you would exercise in choosing a person for a position of trust in the management of your private affairs.

Subject to Action of Democratic Primary
July 28, 1934
3
(Over)

12

PLATE 61

Railroad Commission and General Land Office

The Texas Railroad Commission is made up of three members who are elected on a statewide basis. When the commission was created in late 1891, its purpose was to regulate the railroad industry. The commission was so important and powerful that Senator John H. Reagan came home from Washington to serve as chair of the first commission. With the growth of the oil and gas industry, the commission remained a powerful agency. Since the federal government has taken over regulation of railroads and trucking, the commission's regulatory power has been shrinking in recent years.

The state land commissioner heads the General Land Office, which in early Texas was of great importance to the state. Land was the state's greatest commodity and was used for the public good. Commissioners are elected statewide and also chair the Veterans' Land Board.

1. The son of a lieutenant governor, Beauford Jester (Corsicana), served on the commission from 1942 to 1947. He was elected governor in 1946 with a slogan "With Jester, Texas Comes First."

2. A former mayor of Garland, Charles Matthews served on the commission from 1994 to 2005, when he was appointed chancellor of the Texas State University System.

3. Olin Culberson, who served from 1941 to 1961, used a sewing kit for a giveaway. They were probably quite popular during the Depression.

4. Michael Williams, from Midland, was appointed to the commission by Governor George Bush in 1998. He is the first African American to serve on the commission. He was elected to the post in 2000 and again in 2002.

5. John Sharp, a Democrat, served as a House member and senator before joining the commission in 1986. In 1990, he was elected comptroller and ran unsuccessfully for lieutenant governor in 1998 and 2002.

6. Lena Guerrero's railroad crossing lapel pin leaves little doubt as to the desired office. She was appointed to the commission by Ann Richards and served from 1991 to 1992.

7. Hector Uribe, a former Democratic state senator from Corpus Christi, ran on the platform of abolishing the commission. He lost in 1996.

8. Dan Kubiak, who served in the Texas House, lost this race for land commissioner in the 1982 Democratic primary.

9. Bob Armstrong, an Austin Democrat, was elected to the Land Office in 1972 where he remained until 1982, when he lost a race for governor in the Democratic primary. The guitar-playing attorney later worked in the Department of the Interior during the Clinton administration.

10. Bascom Giles served as land commissioner from 1939 to 1955. He was sentenced to the state penitentiary over his involvement in the Veterans' Land Board scandal in 1956.

11. Garry Mauro, a Democrat, began a yearly cleanup of Texas beaches, thus this "trash" button. He ran unsuccessfully for governor in 1998.

12. J. H. Walker palm card. He served from 1929 to 1937.

PLATE 62

Comptroller, Agriculture Commissioner, and State Treasurer

Like most other Texas offices, the positions of the comptroller, the agriculture commissioner, and the state treasurer (abolished in 1995) are elected. The comptroller keeps the state's books, determines how much revenue is available to the legislature, and collects the state's taxes. The agriculture commissioner regulates most facets of agriculture in the state. The office of state treasurer was abolished by constitutional amendment in November of 1995. The duties were taken over by the comptroller.

1. A palm card for Robert S. Calvert who served as comptroller from 1949 to 1975.

2. Carole Keeton Strayhorn's pin identified the comptroller as "One Tough Grandma."

3. What better campaign advertising than a comb for Agriculture Commissioner Susan Combs?

4. Author and historian Evetts Haley, Jr., made an unsuccessful run for agriculture commissioner.

5. Bill Powers ran for agriculture commissioner in 1986. His bumper sticker featured a chicken, symbolic of the trade association Powers worked for before the election.

6. With a catchy name like Jesse James, this longtime treasurer served from 1941 to 1977.

7. In 1968, the Republican Party ran a state ticket, or "Action Team '68" for several statewide offices. Pictured here are buttons for Sproesser Wynn for attorney general, John Bennett for comptroller, Manuel Sanchez for treasurer, and Millard Neptune for land commissioner.

TEXANS - FORWARD!

ELECT

G. A. JERRY SADLER

Of Gregg County

Railroad Commissioner of Texas

•

**Clean - Honest - Able
Energetic - Fair
Courageous**

•

Young Enough to Look Forward — Not Backward

Experienced Enough to Insure Intelligent, Faithful and Diligent Service

"Put Sadler In The Saddle"

ROBERT S. CALVERT

OF TRAVIS COUNTY

Solicits Your Vote and Influence
For Election to the Office of

State Comptroller

Subject to the Action of the Democratic Primaries

1

2

BENNETT ACTION

SANCHEZ ACTION

7

ELECT
EVETTS
HALEY, Jr.
COMMISSIONER
TEXAS DEPARTMENT
OF AGRICULTURE

4

NEPTUNE ACTION

WYNN ACTION

7

ACTION TEAM **68**

Susan COMBS for Agriculture Commissioner

3

JESSE JAMES

RECENTLY APPOINTED
STATE TREASURER

CANDIDATE FOR
FIRST ELECTIVE TERM

Subject to Action Democratic
Primary, July 25, 1942

(over)

6

Powers
Republican for Agriculture

Pd. Pol. Adv. by Bill Powers Campaign; Ed Small, Treasurer.

5

1

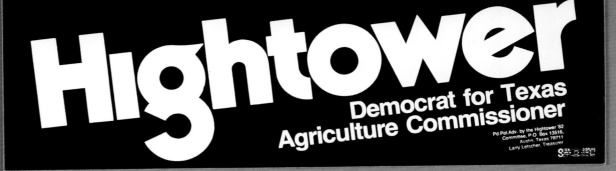

Hightower
Democrat for Texas
Agriculture Commissioner

Pd.Pol.Adv. by the Hightower '82
Committee, P.O. Box 13516,
Austin, Texas 78711
Larry Letscher, Treasurer

HAMBO
PART II

2

NO
MORE
BULL

Hightower
Democrat for
Texas Agriculture
Commissioner

**Enough
is enough!**

Hightower
Democrat for
Texas Railroad Commission

If you eat...
vote for
Hightower
Democrat for
Texas Agriculture
Commissioner

Pd. Pol. Adv. by the Hightower Committee
P.O. Box 13516, Austin, Texas 78711

PLATE 63

Jim Hightower

im Hightower, a political activist and author, first ran for railroad commissioner in 1980, but lost to incumbent Jim Nugent. He was elected agriculture commissioner in 1982 and again in 1986. His buttons show his well-known humor laced with a healthy dose of satire.

1. Bluebonnet seed packets certainly emphasize agriculture.

2. A takeoff on the popular Sylvester Stallone movie. Hightower does not resemble Stallone.

PLATE 64

Rick Perry

efore he became governor, Rick Perry ran for Texas agriculture commissioner. The Texas cowboy image worked, and Perry was elected.

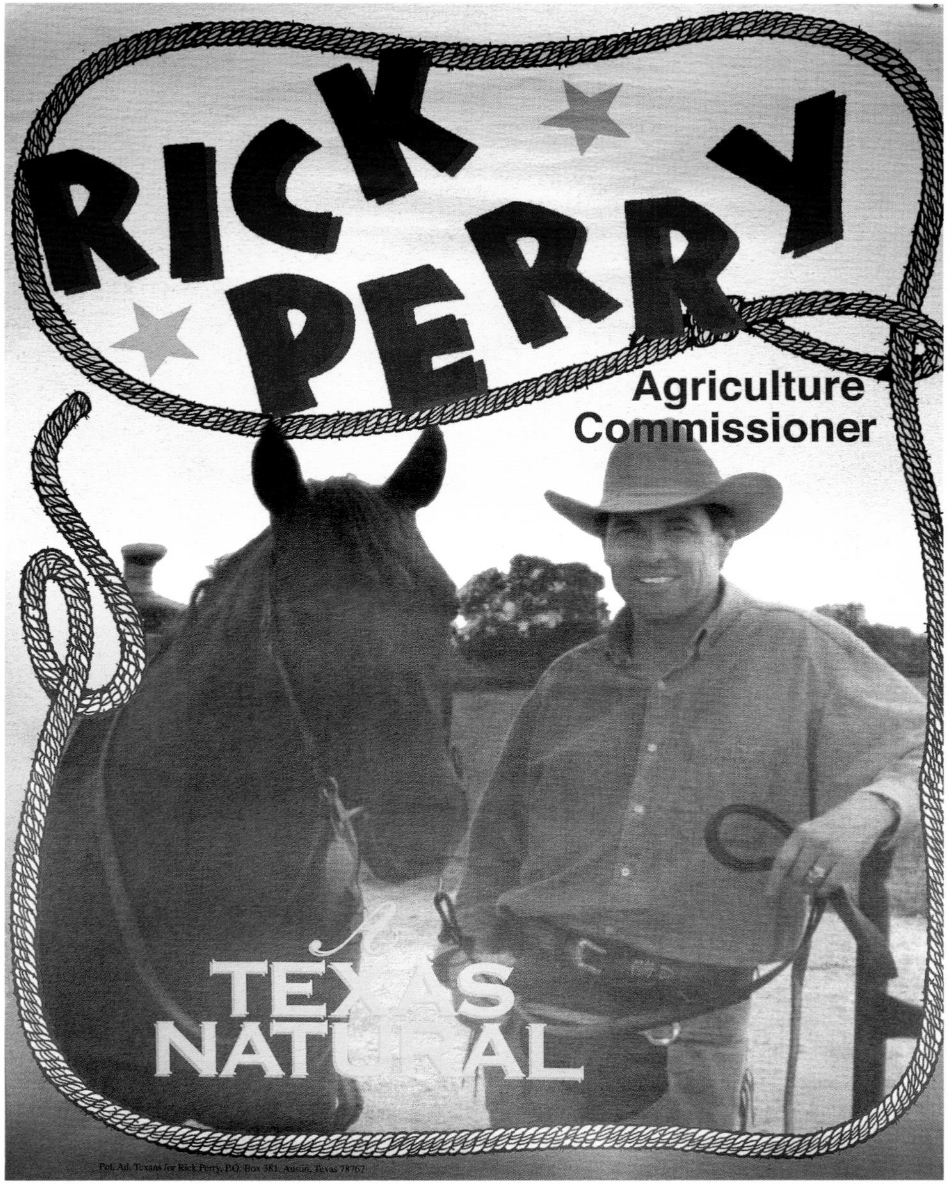

RICK PERRY
Agriculture Commissioner
TEXAS
NATURAL
Pol. Ad. Texans for Rick Perry, P.O. Box 381, Austin, Texas 78767

PLATE 65

State Conventions

Every two years, the state Democratic and Republican parties hold conventions. While most conventions are currently held in the big cities of Houston, Dallas, San Antonio, Austin, and Fort Worth, in earlier years, towns such as Mineral Wells often hosted the parties.

PLATE 66

Appellate Courts

In Texas, there are three appellate courts. The Courts of Appeal (previously Courts of Civil Appeals) are located throughout the state. These courts are the first level of appellate review. There are fourteen such courts, and their justices are elected district-wide. The Supreme Court is the final state appellate court in civil matters, and the Court of Criminal Appeals is the highest criminal appellate court. The members of these last two courts are elected statewide.

1. After years of legal practice and politics, Price Daniel's campaign manager, Joe Greenhill, served as chief justice of the Texas Supreme Court.

2. Morris Overstreet of Amarillo was the first African American on the Court of Criminal Appeals.

3. Tom Phillips served as chief justice on the Texas Supreme Court from 1988 until 2002. He collects political memorabilia and books.

4. This wooden nickel is from Howard Fender, chief justice of the Second Court of Appeals in Fort Worth.

5. Chief Justice Craig Enoch was promoted by the electorate from the Court of Appeals in Dallas to the Texas Supreme Court.

6. Raul Gonzalez, a Democrat, was appointed in 1984 as associate justice of the Texas Supreme Court. He was the first Hispanic so appointed.

7. Democrat C. L. Ray and Oscar Mauzy (a former state senator) were mentioned in the *60 Minutes* story "Justice for Sale." Republicans soon took over the Texas Supreme Court.

8. John Cornyn left the Supreme Court in 1998 when he was elected attorney general. In 2002, he was elected to the U.S. Senate.

9. Bob Gammage served in the Texas House, the Texas Senate, and the U.S. Congress before being elected to the Texas Supreme Court. He ran for governor in 2006.

10. John Onion, Jr., became chief judge of the Court of Criminal Appeals after serving as a district judge in Bexar County.

11. Richard Levy is pictured on an old palm card in his race to serve on the Court of Appeals.

JOE GREENHILL
FOR TEXAS SUPREME COURT

1

OVERCOME WITH OVERSTREET

2

For The Integrity Texans Deserve
Chief Justice Tom Phillips 1988

3

Re-elect Judge John
Cornyn
Texas Supreme Court

8

RE-ELECT
Chief Justice
HOWARD M. FENDER
COURT OF APPEALS

4

RE-ELECT
Judge
C. L. Ray
Texas
Supreme Court

7

BOB
GAMMAGE
Supreme Court

9

RICHARD B. LEVY
OF TEXARKANA, FORMERLY OF LONGVIEW
FOR RE-ELECTION
ASSOCIATE JUSTICE
COURT OF CIVIL APPEALS
SIXTH SUPREME DISTRICT OF TEXAS
WILL APPRECIATE YOUR VOTE AND INFLUENCE
IN THE DEMOCRATIC PRIMARY. JULY 28TH, 1934

11

MEMBER
Chief Justice
Enoch
STEERING
COMMITTEE

5

Vote
Raul
Gonzalez
TEXAS SUPREME COURT

6

Elect
JOHN F. (Jack)
ONION, JR.
JUDGE
CRIMINAL DISTRICT COURT No. 2
BEXAR COUNTY, TEXAS

10

Mauzy
for
CHIEF JUSTICE
TEXAS SUPREME COURT

7

ANNETTE
STRAUSS
for MAYOR of all Dallas

2

MARC
FOR
MAYOR

4

ALEXANDER

MAYOR

5

JOIN US AND ELECT
DUB
ROGERS FOR MAYOR

6

7

I LIKE
MIKE
for
MAYOR of WACO

1

OTHAL BRAND

VOTE
APRIL 4
INTEGRITY
EXPERIENCE
DEDICATION

MAYOR

3

Ron Kirk
FOR DALLAS MAYOR

BOB LANIER
FOR MAYOR

Political advertising paid for by Bob Lanier for Mayor, P. O. Box 272869, Houston, TX 77277-2869

Warning: Placement, posting or erection of this material within the City of Houston is regulated by section 28-38 and 28-39 of the City's code of ordinances and chapter 46 of the City's building code, violation thereof is punishable by a fine of up to $200.

9

RAYMOND
TELLES
For CITY COUNCIL
Pd. Pol. Ad. Jose Angel Silva, Jr., Treas.
1000 S. Stanton, El Paso, TX 79901

8

PLATE 67

City Officers

All mayors and city council members are elected in nonpartisan elections. Mayors are often the face of a city, and the office attracts a large number of capable politicians.

1. Mike Morrisson of Waco.

2. Annette Strauss of Dallas.

3. Othal Brand of McAllen. Mayor Brand was involved in a contentious battle with the United Farm Workers of America in South Texas.

4. Marc Katz of Austin. This well-known restaurateur lost his only race for mayor in 2003.

5. Joyce Alexander of Lockhart.

6. Dub Rogers of Lubbock.

7. Ron Kirk of Dallas. Kirk was defeated for the U.S. Senate by John Cornyn in 2004.

8. Raymond Telles of El Paso.

9. Bob Lanier of Houston.

PLATE 68

City Officers

1. Roy Butler of Austin.

2. Terry Davis of Austin.

3. Mark Rose of Austin. Rose later served as head of the Lower Colorado River Authority.

4. Max Nofziger of Austin. A former street-corner flower salesman, Nofziger surprisingly won a race for city council in the "Live Music Capital" of the U.S.

5. Kay Granger of Fort Worth. Later, Granger was elected to Congress.

6. Jeff Hart of Austin.

7. Mark Spaeth of Austin. Spaeth married Amanda Blake, the actress who played Miss Kitty on *Gunsmoke*.

8. Jeff Friedman of Austin.

9. Carole Keeton McClellan Strayhorn served as mayor of Austin prior to entering state politics.

1

Jeff ❤ Hart
You gotta have Hart.
CITY COUNCIL PLACE 1

Pol. ad pd. for by the Jeff Hart for City Council Campaign, 807 Brazos, Austin, Texas 78701. Martha Smiley and C. Patrick Oles, Jr. Co-Treasurers. This campaign has not agreed to comply with the contribution and expenditure limits of the Austin Fair Campaign Chapter.

6

2

3

8

4

5

SPAETH
City Council Place 4

Pol. adv. pd. for by Mark Spaeth Campaign for City Council, 904 West Ave., Austin, TX 78701.

7

9

1

2

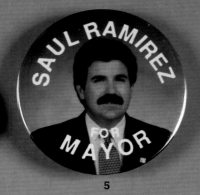

3

4

5

6

7

8

9

10

11

12

13

14

15

16

PLATE 69

City Officials

1. Howard Peak, mayor, San Antonio.

2. Lewis Cutrer, mayor, Houston.

3. Nelson Wolff, mayor, San Antonio.

4. Kathy Whitmire, mayor of Houston, reminded some wags of the movie character Tootsie.

5. Saul Ramirez, mayor, Laredo.

6. Rodney Ellis, city councilman and later state senator, Houston.

7. Jim Clark, mayor, Pasadena.

8. Jack Heard, mayor, former Harris County sheriff, Houston.

9. Jim McConn, mayor, Houston.

10. Lynda Billa Burke, city council member, San Antonio. Lynda used both her married and maiden names, as both her father and father-in-law had served on the San Antonio Council.

11. Henry Cisneros, mayor, later secretary of HUD, San Antonio.

12. Kathy Whitmire, mayor, Houston.

13. Louie Welch, mayor, Houston.

14. Walter Monteith, mayor, Houston.

15. Fred Hofheinz, mayor, Houston. His father, Judge Roy Hofheinz, built the Astrodome.

16. Curtis Graves, mayor, Houston.

PLATE 70

County and District Officials

ike other Texas offices, county and district officials are all elected in partisan races. In rural Texas, prior to the growth of cities, county judges and commissioners were the local political powers. Along with sheriffs, county and district clerks, and tax assessors, county officials were the politicians Texans were most familiar with.

1. Roy Quintanilla for County Court at Law in Galveston County.

2. Wooden nickel supporting Wanda Carter for Gray County clerk.

3. Jose Angel Gutierrez of Zavala County. Gutierrez was one of the founders of La Raza Unida and ran for the U.S. Senate in 1992.

4. Tom Cannon for County Court at Law in Lubbock County.

5. Bob Covington of Guadalupe County. "Maximum Bob" only had misdemeanor jurisdiction as county attorney.

6. E. A. "Squatty" Lyons was a long-serving Harris County commissioner.

7. An older Tarrant County treasurer palm card.

8. Wanda Wray did not win the Lubbock County district attorney race, but her button has a great design.

STERLING 1 2 3 4 5 6

ELECT ROY M. **QUINTANILLA** JUDGE COUNTY COURT # 2

1

Re-Elect
Wanda Carter
County Clerk
Gray County, Texas
DEMOCRAT
There's No Substitute
for Experience

2

RE-ELECT
GUTIERREZ
COUNTY JUDGE

3

CANNON
for
JUDGE

4

MAXIMUM BOB
COVINGTON
COUNTY ATTORNEY

5

I'M FOR
"SQUATTY"
LYONS
PCT. 4
COUNTY
COMMISSIONER

6

*Your Vote and Support Will Be
Appreciated by*
Mrs. Johnnie (Mitt) H..use
Candidate for
COUNTY TREASURER
*who is asking you for Re-Election on
her Qualification, and Efficient
Service Rendered*

SUBJECT TO DEMOCRATIC PRIMARY

7

WANDA
WRAY
DISTRICT
ATTY.

8

VICTOR H.
LINDSEY

Candidate For

DISTRICT JUDGE

72nd Judicial District

COCHRAN — HOCKLEY — LUBBOCK — CROSBY
COUNTIES

Subject to Action of Democratic Primary

1

ELECT THE BEST · FOR A CHANGE

DOUG
WARNE
JUDGE

2

VOTE
WITTIG

6

The man who put it together

ALTON GRIFFIN
The man we need to keep!

3

RE-ELECT
The
RIGHT MAN
JUDGE
SHELLY HANCOCK

4

Elect
PETE
GILFEATHER
County Criminal Court #6

5

PLATE 71

County and District Officials

1. An ink blotter was District Judge Vic Lindsey's choice for political advertising.

2. Family District Court Judge Doug Warne uses refrigerator magnets to advertise his Harris County campaigns. His wife is also a district judge in Harris County.

3. Alton Griffin used emery boards, bumper stickers, and matchbooks in his Lubbock County races for criminal district attorney.

4. The right man for justice of the peace, and later district judge, was Shelly Hancock of Harris County.

5. Pete Gilfeather served as a Criminal County Court judge in Tarrant County.

6. A plastic owl clip for a Don Wittig judicial campaign. A district judge and appellate judge in Houston, Wittig later ran for attorney general against Dan Morales in 1994.

PLATE 72

County and District Officials

1. Steve Ables, a Republican district judge, served as the administrative judge for a large portion of the Hill Country in central Texas.

2. Joe Hart, an Austin district judge, is the son of a former Texas Supreme Court judge.

3. Nattily attired Lewis Brazier ran for re-election as justice of the peace in Potter County.

4. I saw this button in a state agency newsletter and wrote Mr. Joe Brigance, who sent me one of his buttons. You get them any way you can.

5. Emil Macha serves Lamb County, one of the northernmost Texas counties, as county commissioner.

6. Travis County Clerk Dana DeBeauvoir made sure voters could pronounce her name.

7. Like FDR, Bryan Henderson served Tarrant County so long (1949–1968) that he was the only county commissioner many had ever known.

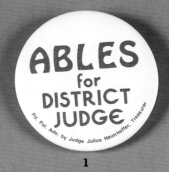

ABLES
for
DISTRICT
JUDGE

Pol. Pol. Adv. by Judge Julius Neunhoffer, Treasurer

1

JUDGE
JOE HART

2

RE-ELECT LEWIS C. BRAZIER

POTTER COUNTY JUSTICE of PEACE

3

Joe
BRIGANCE
COMMISSIONER
BRAZORIA COUNTY

4

!MAchA

5

Dana
DeBEAUVOIR
(Day Bŭv-Wah)

6

Re-Elect

Bryan Henderson

Commissioner

Precinct One

PROVEN ☆ COURTESY ☆ EFFICIENT

36

7

VOTE
For Joel
CLIETT's
Little Brother For
SCHOOL BOARD

1

2

KEEP
Henry
Wade
DA

3

ELECT
JOHN WILEY
PRICE
DEMOCRAT
COUNTY
COMMISSIONER
MAY 5, 1984

4

Paul
Pressler
Judge

5

LARRY
MURDOCH
County Clerk

6

ARCH G. LAMB
County
Commissioner

7

8

vote DEAVER for
D. A.

PLATE 73

County and District Officials

1. Joel Cliett passed these buttons out at his store in San Marcos. His little brother won the seat.

2. One of the earliest-known county buttons is attached to a clip. It is for W. A. Walton, district county clerk of Motley County, dated around 1920.

3. Henry Wade served Dallas County from 1951 to 1987. He is the Wade in Roe v. Wade and prosecuted Jack Ruby in the 1960s.

4. The often-controversial John Wiley Price serves on the Dallas County Commissioners Court.

5. In his non-judicial career, Harris County Judge Paul Pressler led the Southern Baptist Convention.

6. Larry Murdoch of Dallas County held the important post of county clerk. They run most elections in Texas.

7. Arch Lamb, a Lubbock County commissioner, is in all likelihood the only politician in Texas to use Chiclets as a campaign giveaway.

8. Joe Deaver sounds like Beaver, but he lost in Hall County.

PLATE 74

Sheriff

A Texas sheriff is the chief law enforcement officer in Texas's 254 counties. In addition to patrolling the county, most sheriffs also run the county jail and serve process in county and district litigation. An elected official, the sheriff is directly responsible to the voters of each county.

1. C. V. "Buster" Kern served as sheriff in Harris County for many years.

2. L. L. Blaylock used this campaign mirror in Milam County.

3. John Lightfoot served as sheriff in Nacogdoches County.

4. Big Jim Flournoy was the long-time sheriff in Fayette County and was best known for his part in the infamous "Chicken Ranch" story.

5. Lon Evans was a TCU All-SWC guard/tackle and Green Bay Packers football player prior to serving as sheriff.

6. John W. Tobin served as Bexar County sheriff for many years beginning in 1898. This is a whisk broom and button for a clean sweep.

7. Bullet pencil for McLennan County Sheriff W. B. Mobley.

8. Doyne Bailey first served as Travis County Sheriff and then as head of the Texas Alcoholic Beverage Commission.

VOTE FOR
ALEX PEREZ
SHERIFF
CAMERON COUNTY

"I KNOW SAM ALLEN"
ELECT
SAM ALLEN
DALLAS COUNTY
SHERIFF

I AM FOR
TOBIN.
ARE YOU?

6

"LIGHTFOOT"
for
SHERIFF

3

RE-ELECT
★
LON EVANS
SHERIFF

5

I'M FOR
SHERIFF
C.V. BUSTER
KERN

1

4
★★★
RE-ELECT
BIG JIM
SHERIFF
★★★

"ACCEPT THIS MIRROR AS MY CARD"
AND VOTE FOR ME.
L. L. BLAYLOCK
CANDIDATE FOR
SHERIFF
Milam County
YOUR VOTE WILL BE APPRECIATED

2

RE-ELECT
BAILEY
SHERIFF-TRAVIS COUNTY

8

W. B. MOBLEY
FOR SHERIFF

7

"Don't Brush Me Off"
Re-Elect
Sheriff John W. Tobin

6

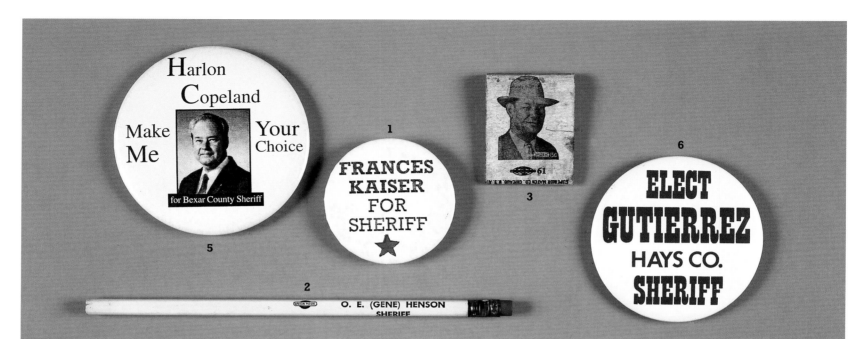

Harlon Copeland
Make Me Your Choice
for Bexar County Sheriff

5

1

FRANCES KAISER FOR SHERIFF

3

61

6

ELECT GUTIERREZ HAYS CO. SHERIFF

2

UNION MADE O. E. (GENE) HENSON SHERIFF

re-elect
RAYMOND FRANK

the Sheriff that shoots straight

1
AMERICAN PRINTERS
EXCHANGE/AUSTIN, TEXAS

Advertisement paid for by Raymond Frank.

4

PLATE 75

Sheriff

1. Frances Kaiser was elected sheriff in Kerr County, becoming one of the few female sheriffs in the country.

2. A pencil for Galveston County Sheriff Gene Henson.

3. Sully Montgomery was sheriff of Tarrant County during the reign of crime along the notorious Jacksboro Highway.

4. Raymond Frank served Travis County as "the sheriff that shoots straight."

5. Harlon Copeland was the longtime Bexar County sheriff.

6. Mr. Gutierrez ran in Hays County.

PLATE 76

Sheriff

Cards from many candidates for sheriff. Owen Kilday of Bexar County made sure you remembered him when he paid your expired parking meter instead of writing you a ticket.

Elect

CHARLIE BOND

Your

SHERIFF

OF BEXAR COUNTY

Qualified By Experience

(OVER)

OWEN W. KILDAY

— FOR —

SHERIFF

Re-elect

Owen W. Kilday

SHERIFF

RE-ELECT

SHERIFF

W.B. "Bill" Hauck

Let's Continue

A Job Well Done

Democratic Primary, May 2, 1964

J. S. McNeel

Candidate for

SHERIFF

Bexar County

Subject to Action of Democratic Primary

July 23, 1932.

YOUR VOTE AND SUPPORT WILL BE APPRECIATED

Elect

Owen W. Kilday

SHERIFF

ANTI-MAVERICK

★★★★★★★★★★★★★★★★★★★★★★★★★★★★★

RE-ELECT

Owen W. Kilday

Your **SHERIFF**

★★★★★★★★★★★★★★★★★★★★★★★★★★★★★

D. E. HAMER

Candidate For

SHERIFF

BEXAR COUNTY, TEXAS

Headquarters Room 217 Lanier Hotel

Subject to the Action of The Democratic Primary July 25th

[over]

ELECT

T. H. (Ted) LACEY

for

SHERIFF

BEXAR COUNTY

Primary July 24, 1948

Will Appreciate your Vote and Support

WILL W. WOOD

CANDIDATE FOR

CONSTABLE

PRECINCT No. 1

BEXAR COUNTY

YOUR VOTE AND SUPPORT WILL

BE APPRECIATED

DEMOCRATIC PRIMARY, JULY 26th, 1930

(OVER)

Help Elect

JESSE WEGENHOFT

your

SHERIFF

of Colorado County

Subject to the Action of the

Democratic Primary July 24, 1954

A. W. WEST, Jr.

CANDIDATE FOR

SHERIFF

Bexar County

*Your Vote will be a Vote For
Honest Law Enforcement*

Subject to Action of Democratic Primary July 28

Your time had

expired . . .

The Red Flag was

showin'

We dropped in a

coin

With the compliments

of Owen!

(A Friend)

WILL W. WOOD

CANDIDATE FOR

SHERIFF

BEXAR COUNTY

Subject to action of Democratic Primary,

July 25, 1936

Your Vote and Support Will Be Appreciated

(OVER)

VOTE FOR

BUCK WHEELER

for

Colorado County Sheriff

Subject to the Democratic Primary, July 24, 1954

YOUR VOTE AND SUPPORT WILL BE GREATLY

APPRECIATED

For Fearless Law Enforcement

ELECT

ALBERT WEST, Jr.

FOR

SHERIFF

Your Vote and Support Will

Be Appreciated

Subject to Action of Democratic

Primary, July 23, 1938

RE-ELECT

OWEN W. KILDAY

Sheriff

BEXAR COUNTY

For Re-Election

Albert Hausser

[SHERIFF]

Over 15 Years Experience

As an Officer, and

Made Good

COURTESY · EFFICIENCY

ECONOMY

RUNNING ON MY RECORD

(over)

W. J. "WILLIE" HAAS

FOR

BLANCO COUNTY

SHERIFF, TAX ASSESSOR-COLLECTOR

YOUR SUPPORT WILL BE APPRECIATED

GENERAL ELECTION · NOVEMBER 7, 1972

2

Gonzalez for GOVERNOR
He's For You!
DEMOCRATIC PRIMARY – JULY 26, 1958

Barbara Jordan
Vice President "76"

LIKE FATHER
LIKE SON
D.C. It Will Be!
Gonzalez
CONGRESS
4

Gonzalez
CONGRESS
4

II BARBARA JORDAN II
KEYNOTE SPEAKER
1992 DEMOCRATIC NATIONAL CONVENTION
1

HENRY
GONZALEZ
1996
20th DISTRICT
for CONGRESS

CONGRESSMAN
KEEP
★ HENRY B. ★
IN D.C.
GONZALEZ

GONZALEZ
FOR CONGRESS
3

Mil Gracias
HENRY B.
Gonzalez
CONGRESS

Keep Henry B in D.C.

PLATE 77

Texas Trailblazers

Before and at the beginning of the civil rights movement, two ambitious, talented, and tough minority politicians made their marks. Henry B. Gonzalez of San Antonio was elected to the Texas Senate in 1957, ran for governor in 1958, and was the first Hispanic elected to Congress from Texas. Upon retirement, his son, Judge Charlie Gonzalez, succeeded him.

Coming out of Houston's tough Fifth Ward, Barbara Jordan was elected to the Texas Senate in 1967. She, too, was elected to Congress, where she gained fame for her eloquent discussion of the U.S. Constitution during the Watergate hearings.

1. This button honored Jordan for being the keynote speaker at the National Democratic Convention in 1976.

2. An early palm card from Gonzalez's run for governor.

3. A tin donkey supporting Gonzalez for Congress. These types of items are called "tabs."

4. One Gonzalez follows another as Henry B.'s son, Charlie, took over the congressional seat after his father retired.

PLATE 78

John Connally

1. Connally was considered as a possible vice presidential candidate in 1976. He made a spirited run for the Republican nomination in 1980 but was easily defeated by Ronald Reagan.

FARENTHOLD
FOR
GOVERNOR
PAID BY JOAN WALES DALLAS
ACTIVE ADV. — DALLAS

SISSY
SI!

SISSY
WILL
CLEAN UP TEXAS

SISSY
SI!

SISSY

SISSY CAN WIN

FARENTHOLD

F
R
A
N
C
E
S
FARENTHOLD

HAVE A NICE ELECTION
FARENTHOLD

1

Frances
FARENTHOLD
for
GOVERNOR

FARENTHOLD
GOVERNOR

SWEEP
CLEAN,
SISSY

12

If preferred, cut along this line to separate into two stickers

FRANCES
Farenthold
GOVERNOR

PLATE 79

Frances "Sissy" Farenthold

Frances "Sissy" Farenthold made a strong run for governor in 1972. She was the first serious female candidate for governor since Miriam "Ma" Ferguson ran in 1932.

1. "Have a Nice Election" is not a slogan that has been used in recent races.

PLATE 80

Dolph Briscoe

Dolph Briscoe, a Democrat, served several terms in the Texas House, beginning in 1949. A rancher/banker from Uvalde, he was elected governor in 1972 and was the first governor to serve a four-year term when he was re-elected in 1974. He lost in the Democratic primary in 1978.

1. A Briscoe door hanger.

2. In 1972, a number of candidates used cloth-covered buttons, such as this red and gold button.

3. This pin was made for Briscoe's staff at the 1972 Democratic National Convention.

4. One of Briscoe's supporters contributed cattle ear-tags, made in several colors, to the campaign.

5. A felt-tip pen used in the governor's office.

6. Pocketknives are rarely used in Texas campaigns.

You Vote for Me and
I'll Work for You.

Dolph

elect
DOLPH
BRISCOE
governor

A man Texans can believe in.

1

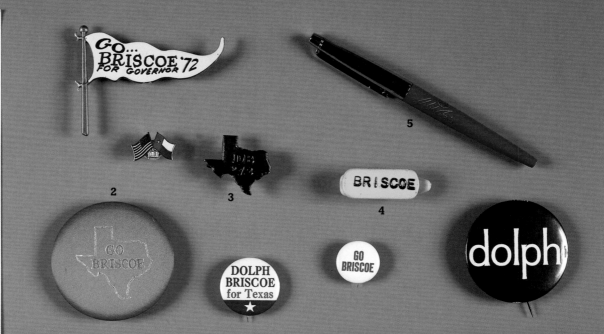

GO...
BRISCOE '72
FOR GOVERNOR

5

2

3

BRISCOE

4

GO
BRISCOE

DOLPH
BRISCOE
for Texas

GO
BRISCOE

dolph

DOLPH BRISCOE · 1978

6

BRISCOE
He kept the promise.

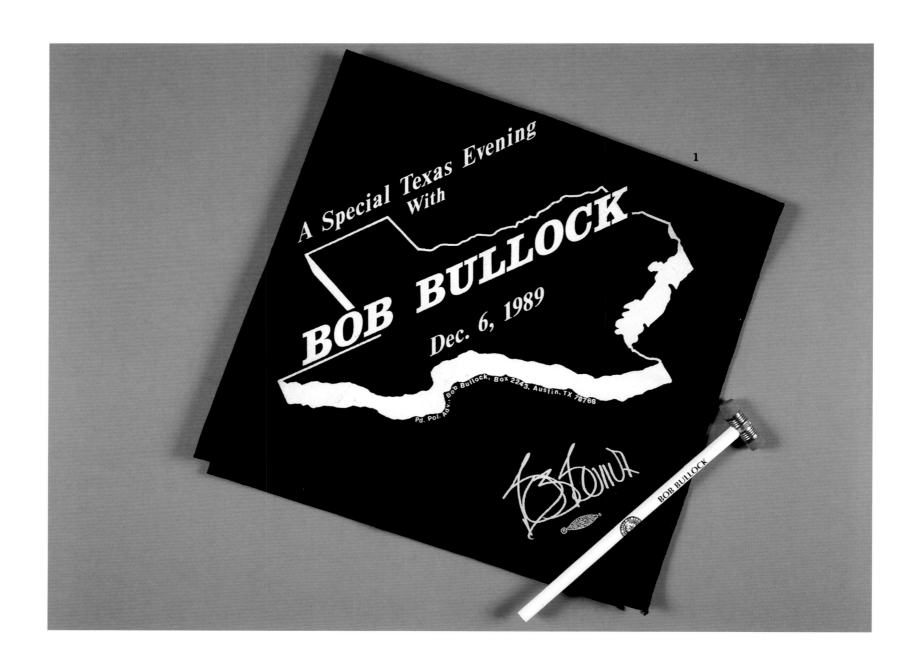

PLATE 81

Bob Bullock

Bob Bullock, a Democrat from Hillsboro, was the last of the old-time Texas political powers. Serving as a House member, Texas secretary of state, comptroller, and lieutenant governor, he understood state government as well as anyone and used this knowledge to do "what was best for Texas."

1. A napkin handed out at an Austin fund-raiser.

PLATE 82

Bob Bullock

1. Button used at a skeet shoot fund-raiser.

2. Bullock ended most of his speeches saying, "God bless Texas." He handed out these stickers and lapel pins while lieutenant governor.

3. This Spanish-language button was produced as a sample but was not used in the campaign.

4. Bullock often talked about running for governor and passed this button out at the 1978 State Democratic Convention.

5. Three "Bullock for lieutenant governor" watches were made.

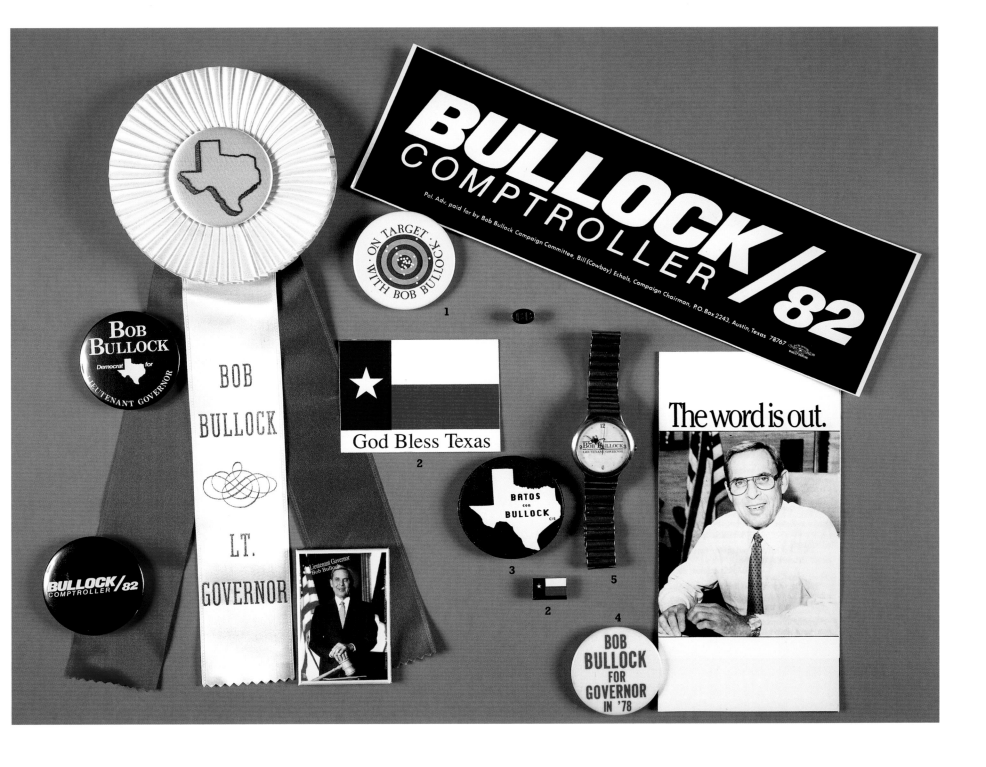

Re-elect
Bill
Hobby
Lieutenant Governor

*A Strong
Lieutenant
Governor . . .
Honestly*

HOBBY
FOR GOVERNOR

Hobby

Hobby

★**Hobby**
LIEUTENANT GOVERNOR

Pol. adv. pd. for by Bill Hobby Campaign, Don Adams,
Treasurer, P.O. Box 567, Austin, Tx. 78767

PAUL
HOBBY
1998
for
STATE
COMPTROLLER

Re-elect
Bill
Hobby
Lieutenant Governor

Political Adv. paid for by Bill Hobby Campaign.
Searcy Bracewell, Treasurer, P.O. Box 567,
Austin, Texas 78767

PLATE 83

Hobby Family

The Hobby family has been active in Texas politics for over a century. Edwin Hobby, the father of Governor Will Hobby, served in the Texas Senate for Woodville County from 1873 until July of 1879.

Governor Will Hobby was elected lieutenant governor in 1914 and again in 1916. Upon the impeachment of Jim Ferguson, he became governor and was elected to that office in 1918.

Will Hobby's son, Bill Hobby, served under Lt. Governor Ben Ramsey as senate parliamentarian in 1959. He was elected lieutenant governor in 1972 and served in that capacity until his retirement in 1990. He held that powerful position longer than any other person.

Bill Hobby's son, Paul, served as executive assistant to Lt. Governor Bullock and ran as the Democratic nominee for comptroller in 1998.

Bill Hobby's maternal grandfather, I. W. Culp, served in the Texas House of Representatives from Bell and Milam Counties. He served with another favorite political father, Sam Johnson, Lyndon's father. I. W. Culp's daughter, Oveta, served as House parliamentarian in 1926, 1929, and 1931. She married Governor Will Hobby and later served as the first secretary of the U.S. Department of Health, Education and Welfare and first commanding officer of the Women's Army Corps.

PLATE 84

The Fergusons

James E. "Pa" Ferguson was elected governor in 1914 and again in 1916. Impeached in 1917 and rebuffed by the Democrats at any attempt for re-election, he supported his wife, Miriam, for election in 1924. She was the first and only female governor until Ann Richards in 1990.

1. A Ma Ferguson inaugural booklet with a dance card included.

2. The *Ferguson Forum* was the political newspaper used by the Fergusons during their campaign.

3. Miriam "Ma" Ferguson. *Jack Wilson Collection.*

4. James E. "Pa" Ferguson.

5. A Roosevelt-Garner-Ferguson button from 1932.

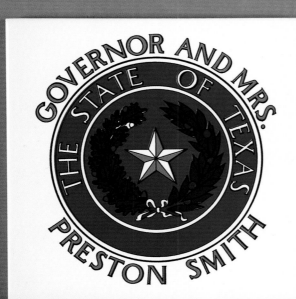

PRESTON SMITH FOR GOVERNOR

1

PRESTON SMITH FOR GOVERNOR

PRESTON SMITH for GOVERNOR

GOVERNOR AND MRS.
THE STATE OF TEXAS
PRESTON SMITH

2

Preston Smith

PRESTON SMITH GOVERNOR

PRESTON SMITH

THE BEST QUALIFIED MAN TO BE GOVERNOR OF TEXAS

SILICONE EYEGLASS TISSUES

3

Preston SMITH for Governor

PRESTON SMITH GOVERNOR

vote for PRESTON SMITH for LIEUTENANT GOVERNOR of Texas

"Working for Texas"

Subject to second Democratic Primary June 2, 1962

PLATE 85

Preston Smith

Preston Smith, a Lubbock businessman, was first elected to the Texas House in 1944. He became Lubbock's senator in 1956 and was elected lieutenant governor in 1962. He served two terms as governor from 1969 to 1973 and left office after the Sharpstown scandal.

1. A cloth-covered red and black button, which, coincidentally, are the Texas Tech colors. Smith was a Tech graduate.

2. A tile with the seal of the state of Texas.

3. A rare political item, eyeglass cleaner.

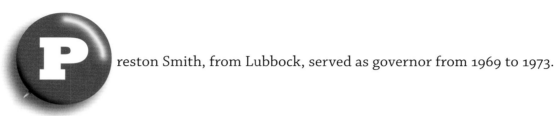

PLATE 86

Preston Smith

Preston Smith, from Lubbock, served as governor from 1969 to 1973.

for
ATTORNEY GENERAL

RALPH

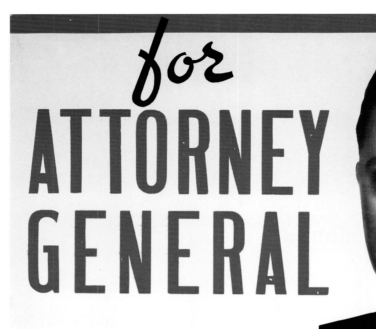

YARBOROUGH

OF TRAVIS COUNTY

- Experienced
  - Capable
    - Energetic
      - Sincere

SUBJECT TO THE DEMOCRATIC PRIMARY

"I Will be Attorney General for the People"

PLATE 87

Ralph Yarborough

Ralph Yarborough ran for attorney general in 1938. Echoing and foreshadowing other attorney general candidates, he portrayed himself as "the people's lawyer."

PLATE 88

Lyndon Johnson

In 1941, Lyndon Johnson lost a special election for U.S. senator to Governor W. Lee O'Daniel. As this colorful poster shows, he pushed his connection with the popular Franklin D. Roosevelt.

LYNDON JOHNSON

U.S. SENATOR

ROOSEVELT ★ UNITY ★ DEFENSE

PLATE 89

John Tower

ohn Tower, U.S. Senator from 1961 to 1989, was known for wearing English-made suits. Stetsons were for the home folks.

PLATE 90

Sam Rayburn

am Rayburn, "Mr. Speaker," represented his East Texas congressional district and was Speaker of the Texas House. He served in Congress from 1912 until his death in 1961, and he held the position of Speaker of the U.S. House of Representatives whenever a Democratic majority controlled the House.

Congressman Sam Rayburn

Re-Election

PLATE 91

Casso March

asso March ran for governor in 1950. Politicians had not yet reached the "no new taxes" level, but a tax-free home was the goal.

PLATE 92

Waggoner Carr

Waggoner Carr, a Democrat from Lubbock, was on the Texas political scene for many years. In his campaigns, he used a wide variety of political items as he ran and won races for state representative, Speaker of the Texas House, and attorney general. He lost a race for the U.S. Senate in 1966 and was preparing a run for governor when he withdrew from politics. As attorney general, he conducted the Texas investigation into the Kennedy assassination and had among his papers the school-book box that was stacked in front of the Texas School Book Depository building window from which Lee Harvey Oswald fired his fatal shots.

1. A ribbon with a metal car was used in the Carr race for Speaker.

2. Stamps used in the 1966 senatorial race.

3. The psychedelic design and colors are unusual in Texas campaigns.

4. A campaign celebration ticket with guest star Jimmy Durante.

5. A palm card from the late 1940s with a "drive in" design.

6. "Viva Carr" button from the 1966 senatorial campaign.

1

2

4

WAGGONER CARR FOR
UNITED STATES SENATOR
VICTORY KICKOFF DINNER

City of Austin
Municipal Auditorium
Monday at 7 PM
September 19, 1966

Nº 8749

FEATURING JIMMY DURANTE

ADMIT ONE · OPTIONAL DRESS

Students
for Waggoner
CARR
for United States
Senate

LET'S GO
WITH
CARR

WAGGONER CARR
for STATE REPRESENTATIVE
PLACE 1, LUBBOCK COUNTY
Democratic Primaries, July 24

5

Vote For
Waggoner Carr
for
GOVERNOR

I'M VOTING FOR
CARR
WAGGONER
FOR
U.S. SENATE

3

CARR
ATTORNEY
GENERAL

Young
Texans for
CARR
for United States
Senator

VIVA CARR

6

a
Democrat
for
Senator!

CARR

Charles WILSON U.S. Congress

JOE BARTON 1996 6th DISTRICT for CONGRESS

OFFICIAL **BARTON BACKER** BUILDER OF "THE FASTEST GROWING REPUBLICAN DISTRICT IN TEXAS" 1988 REPUBLICAN STATE CONVENTION HOUSTON, TEXAS

WILSON

THE **SSC** AND **BARTON BACKERS** Nowhere but the 6th District of Texas

BARTON'S BEST

WILSON

Official **BARTON** BACKER

Re-elect **WILSON**

WILSON GETS IT DONE Charles Wilson for U.S. Congress
Pol. Ad. Pd. for by Wilson For Congress. Comm.
P. O. Box 1930, Lufkin, TX 75901

CONGRESSMAN JOE BARTON **BARTON** Backer CONGRESSIONAL COUNCIL SEMINAR 2-8-92

HE LISTENS TO YOU IN TEXAS **BARTON** Backer HE WORKS FOR YOU IN WASHINGTON

PLATE 93

Two from Texas

Charlie Wilson, from Lufkin, was a popular longtime congressman. Despite a reputation for being a fun-loving playboy, Congressman Wilson is thought by many to have helped defeat the Soviet Union in Afghanistan by his unceasing support for covert operations on an important House committee.

Joe Barton, from Ennis, chairs the powerful Committee on Energy and Commerce in the House. Among his buttons is one supporting the massive but doomed Superconducting Super Collider (SCC), which was built in his district. The House decided in 1993 to halt the project after fourteen miles of tunneling were completed and two billion dollars spent. It was felt that the project was too expensive and that the science could be done elsewhere.

PLATE 94

Two More from Texas

Lubbock's Kent Hance served as state senator and congressman from West Texas. In 1978, he defeated a new politician, George W. Bush, for the congressional seat Hance had inherited from retiring George Mahon. After losing a Democratic U.S. Senate runoff, he changed parties and ran successfully for a seat on the Railroad Commission and unsuccessfully for governor in 1986.

Babe Schwartz, a Democratic state senator from Galveston, served from 1960 to 1981. He was one of the best debaters on the Senate floor, and his debates with Bill Moore of College Station are legendary.

If you've given up looking for courage, independence and leadership in politics... then look again.

KENT HANCE
U.S. SENATE

★ **HANCE**
RAILROAD
COMMISSIONER

RE
ELECT
A. R. **BABE**
SCHWARTZ
SENATOR

CENTURY
KENT HANCE
CLUB

KENT HANCE
FOR
STATE
SENATOR

KENT ★
HANCE
U.S.SENATE

Re-Elect
SCHWARTZ
SENATOR

Babe
Schwartz
For
President

★ **kent**
hance
u.s.
senate

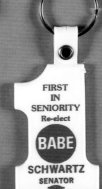

FIRST
IN
SENIORITY
Re-elect
BABE
SCHWARTZ
SENATOR

STERLING   RE-ELECT   A. R. "BABE" SCHWARTZ
STATE SENATOR COASTAL DISTRICT

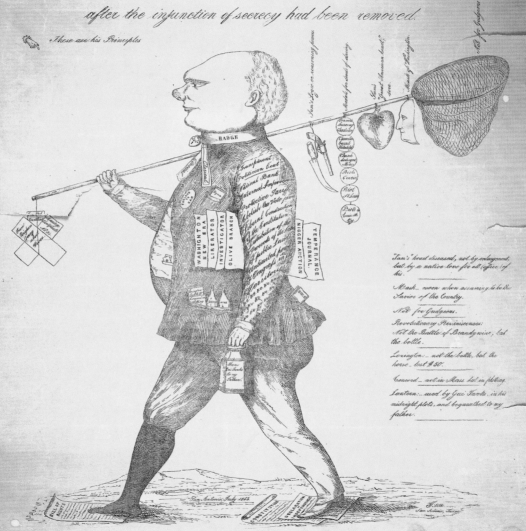

PLATE 95

"Sam Recruiting" Broadside

This broadside "Sam Recruiting" comes as close to a holy grail in Texas political memorabilia as is known. Printed in 1855 by a German printmaker from San Antonio, Wilhelm Thielepape, the lithograph shows Senator Sam Houston, who supported local Know Nothing candidates during this period. The Know Nothings, or the American Party, were neutral on slavery and were generally opposed to immigrants, including the Texas Germans. In *Prints and Printmakers of Texas,* published by the Texas State Historical Association, one can find a detailed description of the various issues and comments found on the print. *University of Texas Center for American History Collection.*

PLATE 96

Mass Meeting, "General Sam Houston" Broadside

The 1860 broadside may well be related to the September 22, 1860, pro-Union meeting held in Austin. While not campaign related, it certainly is political, for at that meeting then-Governor Sam Houston made clear his desire for Texas to remain in the Union. *University of Texas Center for American History Collection.*

MASS MEETING!

SATURDAY, 22d inst.

GEN. SAM HOUSTON,

Will speak in the

HOUSE OF REPRESENTATIVES,

At 11 o'clock, precisely.

FURTHER PROCEEDINGS WILL THEN BE ANNOUNCED.

THE LADIES

are particularly invited.

By order of Com. of Arrang'ts.

❈ ATTENTION ✳ VOTERS! ❈

PLEASE READ THIS.

Anything to beat Hogg. Twenty-five Cents from Wichita Falls to Fort Worth and Return.---Jay Gould.

A Vote for Clark is a vote for Jay Gould.

Texas has had enough of Gouldism. Vote for Hogg and the commission.

Vote for Hogg, the farmers and manufacturer's tried and true friend.

Hogg and Commission. We need both in our business.

It's now or never. Vote for Hogg, the man of and for the people.

It's Gould and Huntington vs. the people. If you are with the people, vote for J. S. Hogg.

Texas has played second fiddle long enough to the Kansas farmer and miller, and the eastern manufacturer. If you are for Texas vote for Hogg and the Commission.

If Clark, Gould, Huntington & Co. are elected, our wheat, like our cotton, will be shipped north and east and we will pay the freight both ways. Vote for Hogg and the Commission if you want more mills and elevators.

25 Cents to Fort Worth and return. Anything to beat Hogg, the people's candidate.---Jay Gould.

Jay Gould has been King of Texas long enough. Vote for Hogg and the Commission.

$2.50 from Fort Worth and Dallas to Houston and return. Anything to beat Hogg.---C. P. Huntington.

Eastern Manufacturers are all fighting Hogg and the Texas commission. This is proof positive that Gov. Hogg is the friend of the people and that we need him and "the" commission in our business.

Vote for Hogg and 'the' Commission

❈ IF YOU ❈

Prefer to pay $20 per thousand for lumber that should be sold at $17, vote for Clark, Gould, Huntington & Co. Hogg and the commission will give you and the railroads justice.

A Commission to regulate the charges to be made by teamsters for hauling over the public roads would be as equitable and legitimate as a commission to fix rates on the railroads.—Gazette, Clark Organ, Nov. 4, '92. With "teamsters on public roads" we have competition, with Texas railroads we have a combination. Hence it is necessary to have the railroad commission. Vote for Hogg and we will have what is due us and Texas and her people will prosper.

FARMERS have made Wichita Falls what she is to-day. We want more of them. Hogg and "the" commission will settle Northwest Texas with good people.

SPECIAL TRAIN from Dallas to Fort Worth Nov. 5th, account of Clark rally. Anything to beat Hogg.—Jay Gould.

ON THE PRICE of freight rates depends the price of grain, and on the price of grain depends the value of land and town property. Hence the importance of "the" commission and having a man like Gov. Hogg for governor.

$74,000,000 increase in Texas values. "Hogg has ruined Texas." On with the ruin. Vote for Hogg.

THIS MAN

Is in Texas to stay and it is to the interest of all who intend to make Texas their home that he (the farmer) be considered and that he be given a fair freight rate Re-elect Governor Hogg and the farmer will be given justice.

If You are interested in the Kansas farmer and miller and the eastern manufacturer, vote for Clark, Gould & Co.

If you are interested in Wichita county and Texas, vote for Hogg and the commission.

If You prefer to use Kansas and Michigan salt and flour to that of Texas, vote for Clark, Gould & Co.

THE Commission is what the people want and voted for. Clark, Gould & Co. have fought the commission from the start.

Gov. Hogg, A Man of and for the People; VOTE FOR HIM

John Howard

PLATE 97

"Vote for Hogg and 'the' Commission" Broadside

This 1892 broadside from Wichita Falls supports the election of Governor Jim Hogg and the creation of a Railroad Commission. The quote beneath the seal is from railroad tycoon Jay Gould, who obviously opposed Governor Hogg and his attempts to regulate the railroad industry. *University of Texas Center for American History Collection.*

PLATE 98

The Politicians in Hot Water

This political play from the late 1870s satirizes the politicians of the day. The main character is James W. Throckmorton, a Democrat who was elected governor in 1866 only to be removed by Republican Reconstructionists the following year. In the 1870s, he made another unsuccessful run at the governorship.

Richard Coke was elected governor in 1873 but nearly had to resort to force to remove the Reconstructionist Republican governor, Edmund Davis, from the old Capitol building.

John Ireland was elected governor in 1882 and re-elected in 1884. During his term, the University of Texas was funded and the cornerstone for the current Capitol was laid.

This "political" play makes it clear that during the late 1870s the Democratic Party was made up of many parts, and that the lack of a prominent Republican Party did not mean a lack of political feuds. *University of Texas Center for American History Collection.*

The POLITICIANS in HOT WATER

Or Drinks All Around!

A Tragi-Comedy in Two Acts!

DRAMATIS PERSONEL.

Col. Ephriam Smooth, a Throckmorton Democrat.
Gen. I. M. Whatisay, a Coke Democrat.
Maj. Bogus Granger, an Ireland Democrat.
Hon. J. H. Backpay, a Democratic Member of Congress.

ACT I. SCENE 1.

[PLACE: The back office of the "Back Pay" Member of Congress, where a consultation of leaders is held to settle the policy of the party for the time being and to determine who the caucus shall nominate as the "delegate from Travis county" to the Constitutional convention. TIME: Ten o'clock at night.]

Col. Ephriam Smooth: Now, as we have met by appointment to settle the preliminaries, we must have a free and confidential expression of opinions both as to measures and men. We must be frank and speak out. To begin, What does our friend Major Bogus Granger think of the situation of affairs?

Major Bogus Granger: Why, it's bad enough. There is no use to conceal the truth among ourselves.

Gen. I. M. Whatisay: I don't understand you. Is not everything going on very well? Gov. Coke's administration has reduced the taxes and is practising retrenchment and reform in all directions except as to the heads of departments, the Legislature, etc. What makes you take a gloomy view of our prospects?

Major Bogus Granger: That sort of twaddle will do well enough for the public; our newspapers have a sufficient supply of it on hand for all occasions and deal it out rather too lavishly, but it won't go down with the people. You know as well as I do that Coke's administration has proven a failure, and, what is worst of all, a *costly failure*. When we compare the figures in the Comptroller's Report of 1868 with those in Coke's two general messages, as Col. Glenn did at the late Radical convention, it is clear from Coke's own showing that our public debt increased only six hundred thousand dollars during the five years when Pease and Davis were governors, and that during Coke's first year it increased to over three and one-half millions dollars! Then by footing up the appropriations in the general laws of the fourteenth Legislature; *and not counting those in the Speeial Laws*, it cannot be denied that our *Reform Legislature* besides

1

Inauguration of
Governor
W. Lee O'Daniel
and
Lieutenant Governor
Coke R. Stevenson
January 21, 1941

Chairman
BARBECUE

2

UVALDE
HOME OF
GOV. DOLPH BRISCOE

**TEXAS
INAUGURATION**
★
1973

3

HE'S THE
SAME
SAFE
COLQUITT

IT'S THE
SAME
OLD
MENARD

4

**THE
PEOPLE'S
CHOICE
FOR
U. S.
SENATOR**

5

**RE-ELECT
TOWER
U. S. SENATOR**

6

PLATE 99

Texas Rarities

The following campaign items are unusual and rare.

1. The ribbon was worn by a barbeque chairman at Governor O'Daniel's famous inaugural barbeque on the grounds of the State Capitol. *Jack Wilson Collection.*

2. Governor Dolph Briscoe became Uvalde's second famous politician after John Nance Garner. This button is from his hometown. *Jack Wilson Collection.*

3, 4. O. B. Colquitt served as governor from 1911–1915 and ran unsuccessfully for U.S. senator in 1916. The "same old Menard" may refer to Menardville, which changed its name to Menard so that the Fort Worth and Rio Grande Railroad would have an easier time painting its signs as it moved into the county. *University of Texas Center for American History Collection.*

5. This is an unusual rebus re-election button for John Tower. *Jack Wilson Collection.*

6. Price Daniel, Sr., ran for the U.S. Senate in 1952. His campaign buttons are almost nonexistent. *Jack Wilson Collection.*

PLATE 100

Texas Rarities

he following Texas-related presidential campaign items are rare and unusual:

1. Texas collector Jack Wilson often combs out-of-the-way places in a quest for political items. In East Texas, he found this Roosevelt-Garner rarity showing the Democratic team offering to help Texas out of the Depression. It is probably the most unique Texas button. *Jack Wilson Collection.*

2. This 1964 porcelain button supporting Barry Goldwater is probably handmade. *Jack Wilson Collection.*

3. Another extremely rare East Texas find is this "Tyler Commercial College for Woodrow Wilson" button. *Jack Wilson Collection.*

4. In 1928, New York Governor Al Smith ran for president on the Democratic ticket. This paper ribbon is from that campaign. *Jack Wilson Collection.*

5. Judson Harmon, an Ohio senator, ran for the Democratic presidential nomination in 1912. This button is from his Texas campaign. *University of Texas Center for American History Collection.*

6. A number of states had Taft First Voters Clubs. This button is from the Texas Club. *Jack Wilson Collection.*

7. In 1901, President William McKinley visited Houston. This ribbon came out of the Mrs. Anson Jones collection. She was the widow of the last president of the Republic of Texas. *University of Texas Center for American History Collection.*

1

2

3

TEXAS
FOR

AL SMITH

4

5

6

HOUSTON
TEXAS.

RECEPTION
COMMITTEE

IN HONOR OF
PRESIDENT McKINLEY
AND PARTY

....MAY 3, 1901....

7

John Doctoroff
DALLAS

GEORGE C. BUTT
FOR GOVERNOR
on November 4th
Vote for an Honest Administrat

PLATE 101

George C. Butte Poster

George C. Butte was a lawyer, an expert on public utility laws, and dean of the U.T. Law School. In 1924, he ran on the Republican ticket against Miriam "Ma" Ferguson to no avail. *Jack Wilson Collection*.

PLATE 102

Charley Lockhart Poster

harley Lockhart served as Texas treasurer from 1931 to 1941. *Texas State Library and Archives Commission.*

CHARLEY
LOCKHART

REWARD FAITHFUL SERVICE

CANDIDATE FOR RE-ELECTION

State Treasurer

Subject to Action Democratic Primary, July, 23, 1938

Vol.I. "*Go Ahead!*" No.3.

Davy Crockett's
18 ALMANACK, 37
OF WILD SPORTS IN THE WEST,
Life in the Backwoods, & Sketches of Texas.

O KENTUCKY! THE HUNTERS OF KENTUCKY!!!

Nashville, Tennessee. Published by the heirs of Col. Crockett.

PLATE 103

Davy Crockett's
Almanac of Wild Sports, 1837

After losing his congressional seat in 1835, Congressman Crockett supposedly told a crowd of Tennessee voters that "You can go to hell, I am going to Texas." And to Texas he went, to die at the Alamo, March, 1836. Davy Crockett Almanacs are not campaign items. Indeed, they were published into the 1840s, well after his death. They are political in the sense that they portray a former elected official as a man of the people, a man who died for his new country, and a man who said, "Be sure you are right, then go ahead." *Texas State Library and Archives Commission.*

PLATE 104

Texas Mementos

1. In Bill Crawford's book about W. Lee O'Daniel, *Please Pass the Biscuits, Pappy*, a vendor at the O'Daniel inaugural is seen selling pennants which look identical to this one.

2. Pennants for Governors Bush and Briscoe.

3. "Wake Up, America!" recording for John Connally's 1980 presidential campaign.

4. A fund-raising memento pen from Bob Bullock.

5. A Mark White inaugural plate. Another plate from the same set is in the Governor's Mansion collection of gubernatorial gifts.

6. *A Texan Looks at Lyndon*, written by noted Texas historian J. Evetts Haley, was a bitter attack on fellow Texan LBJ.

2 Bush

4

2 BRISCOE

3 CONNALLY
LEADERSHIP FOR AMERICA
"WAKE UP, AMERICA!"
A song for the John Connally For President
campaign written by Sharon Barberly Aamesen,
music by Judy Barberly Aamesen.
STEREO   33 1/3 rpm

5

6 A TEXAN LOOKS AT LYNDON
Study in illegitimate power
J. Evetts Haley

1 INAUGURATION
AUSTIN, TEXAS JANUARY 17, 1939
GOVERNOR W. Lee O'Daniel

PLATE 105

Texas Mementos

1. A bust of Governor Miriam Ferguson, probably issued for the inaugural in 1925.

2. This Dolph Briscoe lunch-bucket contained a fund-raising meal and was available in both black and orange.

3. According to George H. W. Bush's friend Patricia Allday, Barbara Bush did the needlework on this purse for her husband's 1964 campaign for U.S. Senate.

4. Author Booth Mooney penned this campaign biography for Coke Stevenson in 1947.

5. Mark White bricks from the Butler Brick Co. in Austin.

6. A Franklin Roosevelt cigar box from the Cuban Cigar Company in Austin.

7. A "Jack Hightower for Congress" gimme cap.

8. A plastic Ann Richards mug.

PLATE 106

T-shirts and Ties

1. Lt. Governor Ben Barnes lost in the Democratic Primary in 1972.

2. Sissy Farenthold made the runoff in the 1972 Democratic primary but eventually lost to Dolph Briscoe.

3. Jeff Friedman, the "boy mayor," was in his twenties when he was elected Austin's mayor in 1975.

4. The *Austin American-Statesman*'s political cartoonist Ben Sargent drew the cartoon on this Killer Bees T-shirt commemorating the quorum-busting state senators in 1979.

5. This "All the Way with L.B.J." tie in burnt orange and white was sold at Joseph's Men Shop on Congress Avenue in Austin.

6. A Waggoner Carr tie from his U.S. Senate race.

BEN BARNES FOR GOVERNOR

1

2
Frances
Farenthold
for Governor

FEARLESS FRIEDMAN FOLLOWER
mayor '75

3

ALL THE WAY WITH L.B.J.

5

SENATOR CARR

6

66th Legislature
The Killer Bees!

4

Index

Page numbers in *italics* refer to illustrations.

Acknowledgments

After 45 years of collecting, it is probably impossible to remember everyone who brought a button or other political item for my collection. But, I will try. From my family, thanks to my mother, Betty Petersen, my dad, Clement Bailey, my brothers, David and Kevin Bailey, my father- and mother-in-law, George and Peggy Crews, my wife's grandmother and great aunt, Viola Banner and Ruby Sloan, my wife's aunt and uncle, Alice and Bob Banner, and their son, Baird Banner. Also thanks to my aunt and uncle Jim and Gladys Willis, their daughter Ginny Willis, and my uncle Charles Willis, my great aunt, Duma McDonald, and my grandparents O. B. and Verna King.

From my friends, John Zihlman, Judge Tom Cannon, Jimmy Frank Davis, Judge E. H. Boedeker, Dr. Kenneth Davis, Dr. Jim Harper, Dr. Roger Aertker, Tom Sawyer, Abigail Thomason, Congressman Kent Hance, Harvey Morton, Governor Preston Smith, Judge J. Q. Warwick, Alton Griffin, Betty Quimby, Carl and Jo Pierce, John and Cindy Cantwell, Jack and Beth O'Donnell, Stephen Rosales, Lt. Governor Bob Bullock, Jan Bullock, Charlie Russell, Colonel Dudley Thomas, Chief Floyd Hacker, Norman Suarez, Wallace Nelson, Dr. David and Diana Carr, Jack Wilson, Drew Julian, George Myers, Freddie Warner, Buddy Jones, David and Dealy Herndon, Senator Babe Schwartz, Speaker Bill Clayton, Speaker Gib Lewis, Debbie Mitchell, Debra Gray, Cay Greene, Wardaleen Belvin, Senator Rodney Ellis, Lt. Governor Bill Hobby, Larry Craddock, Larry Milner, Dan Pearson, Jay Howard, Senator Kim Brimer, Senator Judith Zaferrini, State Representative Chuck Hopson, State Representative Delwin Jones, Ralph Wayne, Speaker Pete Laney, Barry Miller, Chief Justice Tom Phillips, State Representative Willis and Patti Whatley, Secretary of State David Dean, Secretary of State Roger Williams, Larry Beauchamp, Governor Rick Perry, Joyce Sibley, Joe Allbaugh, Barry McBee, Treasurer of the United States Azie Taylor Morton, Senator Joe Christie, Gaylord Armstrong, Secretary of the Senate Betty King, Barbara Schlief, Mayor Mike Moncrief, Secretary of State John Fainter, Russ Johnson, Farley Katz, Art Troilo III, Brad Gabbert, Jerry Bobbitt, Jerry Oxford, Wade Anderson, State Representative Mike Millsap, Judge Jack Hightower, Chris and Paula Conley, Doug and Susan Hill, Judge Doug Warne, Dr. David Ammons, Jim Loyd, Frances and Terry Goodman, Becky Levy, Charles Evans, Bob Johnson, Mike Toomey, Donna Brown, Secretary of State George Bayoud Asst. Senior Texas Ranger Captain Skippy Rundell, Senator Ray and Mary Margaret Farabee, Charlie Simpson, Lucy Glover, Dr. Caryl Dalton, Sue Kelly, Kim Baldwin, Congressman Joe Kilgore, Congressman Jake Pickle, Mary Young, Susan Longley, Mary Anne Wiley, John Somyak, Mike Fields, Joe Fletcher, Chester Alexander, Tom Huebner, Carolene English; Ben Rogers, Judge Leon Douglas, Reverend Jim Coley, Mark Lehman, Senator Pete Snelson, Charlotte Nacozy, Charlie Babb, Joe Babb, Karen Ramming, Mike McKinney, Mark Weiss, Christina Mendoza, Betty Salinas, Patti Schwertner, Faye Carson, Simi Denson, Lynda Burke, Pat and Marcia Hubbard, Jim Boynton, Elaine Johnstone, A. J. Jundi, Senator Ralph Yarborough, B. L. Parker, Claudia Stravato, Byrn Bass, Loretto Espinosa, Gloria Turner, Chancellor Charles Matthews, Sandy Senter, Jane Churchill, Brian Graham, Ken Olsen, Joe Gunn, Dr. Cindy Rugely, Joy Anderson, Wally Scott III, Duke Bodisch, Laura McElroy, Harriet Burke, James Cribbs, Tony Profitt, Carleton Turner, Glen Hunt, Chancellor John Montford, Mickey Bently, Nancy Molleda, Harvey Kronberg, Tom Harrison, Judge Charles Scott, David Hess, Jack Roberts, Drew Durham, Arletta Caruthers, T. Getterman, Stroud Kelly, Skip Smith, Commissioner Bob Armstrong, Commissioner Jerry Patterson, Mickey Dorsey, Jim Phillips, Senator Hector Uribe, Bill Powers, Phyllis Thomas, Beva Burdick, Mark Heckman, Commissioner Michael Williams, Mike Morrisey, Jim Word, Jim Shearer, Deanna DeCuffa, Bert Hurlburt, Mark Harkrider, Sara Woelk, State Representative David Counts, John Lorenzi, Randy DeLay, State Representative Paul Colbert, Judge Bob Hughes, Zant Woodul, Sheriff Choc Blanchard, Ranger Captain Dub Clark, Senator Florence Shapiro, Senator Jane Nelson, Dianna Lolley, Judge Steve Martin, Jeff Bonham, Senator Kent Caperton, Johnnie B. Rogers, Jr., Senator Bill

Haley, Chuck Rice, State Representative Barbara Rushing, Jack Chappell, Priscilla Bishop, State Representative Parker McCullough, Bill Todd, State Representative Dale Tillery, Monte Williams, Doug Miller, Bill Heatly, Jr., Chief Joe Cook, Judge John McFall, County Clerk Larry Murdoch, Forrest Smith, Van Vannerson, Chuck Hempstead, Peary Perry, Richard Crozier, Texana Conn, Rick Jacobi, Cliff Morton, Richard Craig, Peggy Smith, Ben Sarrett, Mike Hodge, George Korbel, Lynda Nessenholtz, Dr. John Rogers, Max Noe, Sharon Weintraub, Margaret Vollers, Burke Randolph, Greg Wilson, Lacy Gourly, Kerry Grombacher, Roger Easterday, Glen Castlebury, and Governor Dolph Briscoe.

Also, I'd like to thank Steve Bresnen, Paul Burns, Walter Johnson, Donna Roming, Buck Wood, Shelley Smith, Carolyn Busch, Ranger Wallace Spillar, John Kinney, Bob Strauser, Ashley Estes, Bob Binder, Ranger Joe Peters, Jeff Heckler, Bill Wischkaemper, Mary Jane Manford, Jim Hargrove, Cecelia Burke, Tom Sonnenberg, Larry Todd, Danny Burger, Susan Hill, Senior Ranger Captain Bill Wilson, Terry Ryan, Scott McClellan, Forrest Fenn, Colonel Tommy Davis, Julia Hartley, Jack Wilhelm, Peggy Romberg, Bill Bownds, Ginger Samuelson, Betty Naylor, Fred Lewis, Bonnie Parott, Wayne T. Franke, Laurie Rich, State Representative Tracey King, Glen Castleberry, and Dr. George Shipley.

Thanks to my colleagues on the book, my co-author, Bill Crawford, a true man of ideas and photographer Barbara Schlief who was never satisfied with anything but the best. Thanks also to Bill Bishel at U. T. Press, Steve Williams at the U. T. Center for American History, and Chris LaPlant and John Anderson at the Texas State Archives and Library. Also thanks to Carole Gambill, who deciphered my handwriting and my colleagues at Strasburger & Price who always wonder what I really do for a living. A special thanks to my friend, Jack Wilson, who shared his wonderful collection.

Most especially I thank my daughters Sara and Catherine who are wise beyond their years and my wife Susan, to whom I listen more than she knows.